D1297625

Sound and Poetry

Sound and Poetry

ENGLISH INSTITUTE ESSAYS · 1956

EDITED WITH AN INTRODUCTION BY *Northrop Frye*

COLUMBIA UNIVERSITY PRESS

NEW YORK AND LONDON

WILLIAM MADISON RANDALL LIBRARY UNC AT WILMINGTON

Copyright © 1957 Columbia University Press

First printing 1957
Third printing 1967

Library of Congress Catalog Card Number: 57–11003
Printed in the United States of America

PE 1010
.E5
1956

Preface and Acknowledgments

THIS BOOK includes the papers presented at two con-
ferences of the English Institute. The editor's introduction [1] and
the three following papers were read at the 1956 conference on
"Music and Poetry," directed by Mr. Sternfeld of Dartmouth
College (now of Oxford University). The next three papers were
read at the 1955 conference on "Sound and Meaning in Poetry,"
directed by Mr. Victor M. Hamm of Marquette University. A
fourth paper in the same conference, "Prosody and Musical
Analysis," by Mr. Hollander of Harvard University, may be
found in the *Journal of Aesthetics and Art Criticism,* 1956.

In Mr. Sternfeld's paper, the only one which employs quota-
tions not in the public domain, the passages from *Ulysses* and
Dubliners are quoted with the permission of Random House,
Inc., the poems from Yeats with the permission of the Macmillan
Company, and the passages from *Finnegans Wake* with the per-

---

[1] This paper contains material drawn from an early article, "Music
in Poetry," *University of Toronto Quarterly,* 1942. It is this article that
Mr. Sternfeld is quoting on p. 38.

162628

mission of Viking Press, Inc. The page references in his quotations are to the editions listed here.

Although this book is technically a collection of essays, the
reader will find it a well unified and logically developed volume.
The unity comes, not from formal agreement—no one who has
ever attended an English Institute conference would expect or
want such agreement—but from the unconscious logic of scholarship itself, which has produced—to extend the musical metaphors
of the opening papers—a set of six variations on a central theme.
The editor's introduction, though originally one of the papers
contributed, is now best read as an attempt to indicate something
of the scope and importance of that theme, as worked out from
six scholarly points of view: those of musical composition, of
musicological criticism, of musicological history, of rhetoric, of
rhetorical analysis, and of linguistics. To say that the editor is
indebted to his six colleagues for making such a book possible
would be a most proper academic understatement.

N. F.

Contents

page *ix* INTRODUCTION: LEXIS AND MELOS
by *Northrop Frye*

Part One: The Poetry of Sound

3 WORDS INTO MUSIC: THE COMPOSER'S APPROACH
TO THE TEXT
by *Edward T. Cone*

16 POETRY AND MUSIC—JOYCE'S ULYSSES
by *Frederick W. Sternfeld*

55 MUSICA MUNDANA AND TWELFTH NIGHT
by *John Hollander*

Part Two: The Sound of Poetry

85 STRUCTURE, SOUND, AND MEANING
by *Craig La Drière*

109   SPENSER AND MILTON: SOME PARALLELS AND CONTRASTS
        IN THE HANDLING OF SOUND
        by *Ants Oras*

134   FROM LINGUISTICS TO POETRY
        by *Harold Whitehall*

147   SUPERVISING COMMITTEE, THE ENGLISH INSTITUTE, 1956

148   THE PROGRAM, 1956

151   REGISTRANTS, 1956

Introduction: Lexis and Melos

EVER SINCE Lessing in the *Laokoön* warned against the dangers of illegitimate analogies among the arts, critics have tended to think that all such analogies are suspect—a most lame and impotent conclusion. It is of course clear that many of the superficial analogies are either misleading or pointless. To describe one art in terms of another is a stock rhetorical device of little importance. We are familiar with the poet who feels that his poem will look more impressive if he calls it a symphony, and with the composer who feels that his piece will gain in suggestiveness if he calls it a tone poem. Such literary titles as *Triple Fugue* or *Christmas Oratorio* are flourishes of the same kind; *Point Counterpoint* and *Four Quartets* may be more deeply significant, but the nature of the significance has yet to be established. Some musical forms certainly can be imitated in words up to a point: it is quite practicable to write a story, as Thomas Mann did, in some kind of literary analogy to the sonata form, and the variation structure suggests a number of literary analogues, ranging from *The Ring and the Book* to *Thirteen Ways of Looking at a Blackbird*.

Such imitations are by no means a recent invention. That wonderful thirteenth-century contest of wryteling and gogeling, *The Owl and the Nightingale,* has much of what would later be called divisions on a ground in its structure, and a later *tour de force,* Crashaw's *Musicks Duell,* imitates the baroque aria with instrumental accompaniment which was its musical contemporary. Joyce, for all his detachment about Wagner, uses the Wagnerian leitmotiv in the "Sirens" chapter of *Ulysses,* and could perhaps never have worked out the techniques of *Finnegans Wake* without some Wagnerian influence. But it is difficult to know what to say about such imitations beyond observing the fact that they exist. The same may be said of other relationships which seem to me genuinely significant, such as the relation of allegory to counterpoint. For the important but little investigated question of how the rhythm of music may suggest rhythms of verse, I refer you to Mr. Sternfeld's paper and to his *Goethe and Music* (1954), which is not only a fascinating book in itself, but what our friends in the social sciences would call a pilot study.

Melos, lexis, and opsis; music, diction, and spectacle, are three of the six aspects of poetry listed by Aristotle. In drama, which is what Aristotle had chiefly in mind, the relation of melos and opsis to poetry is easily dealt with: melos means actual music and opsis the actual scenic effect. I am concerned here with a slightly different question, the question of what affinities to music may be discerned in the features that poetry shares with music—sound and rhythm. I recognize two types of poetic melos in this sense of the term.

My first objective is to establish an intelligible meaning for the term "musical" in literary criticism. By "musical" I mean a qual-

ity in literature denoting a substantial analogy to, and in many
cases an actual influence from, the art of music. It is perhaps
worth mentioning, at the risk of being obvious, that this is not
what the word ordinarily means to the literary critic. To him it
usually means "sounding nice." Tennyson, for instance, is hailed
by many of his critics as musical; Browning is frequently called
unmusical, as I understand he was by Tennyson. Yet it would
be hard to find a poet who was less likely to be influenced by
music than Tennyson, or a poet who took a more constant and
intelligent interest in the art than Browning. The term musical
as ordinarily used is a value term meaning that the poet has
produced a pleasant variety of vowel sounds and has managed to
avoid the more unpronounceable clusters of consonants that
abound in modern English. If he does this, he is musical, whether
or not he knows a whole note from a half rest.

The reasons for this curious semantic development are full of
interest. One of them takes us back to the literary metaphor about
music that we see in the words "harmony" and "concord." Harmony in its non-musical sense means a stable and permanent
relationship, and in this sense of the word, there is no harmony
in music at all: music is not a sequence of harmonies, but a
sequence of discords ending in a harmony. Music does not attain
literary harmony until it reaches its final tonic chord and is all
over: until then, even the tonic chord in root position would still
be made discordant by the form of the music, which demands
more music to complete its resolution. Browning's "Why rush
the discords in, but that harmony should be prized?" is, unlike
most of Browning's allusions to music, an unmusical literary
man's comment. If we prize harmony we should not start any

music going at all, for every piece of music is a disturbance of an underlying concord. Milton's remark about contrapuntal music in *L'Allegro* as: "Untwisting all the chains that tie/ The hidden soul of harmony," is a much more genuinely accurate one.

In literature one often sees the literary meaning of harmony attached to the music of the unfallen world. In *At a Solemn Musick* Milton tells us how the "disproportioned chime" of sin broke the "perfect diapason" of the state of good, to which we are to return in heaven. This conception of "perfect diapason" is all very well as a literary metaphor, but when translated into music it opens up the discouraging prospect of spending the whole of eternity screaming the chord of C major. Music itself, when it depicts ethereal bliss, generally does so in elementary diatonic chords: Haydn's "The Heavens are Telling," Handel's Hallelujah Chorus, Beethoven's "Glory of God in Nature," assure us that in heaven all tears are wiped from human eyes and all dominant sevenths promptly resolved. On the other hand, the "Representation of Chaos" with which Haydn's *Creation* begins tells us much more about the resources of music itself: like Milton's Satan, it shows us that human art is considerably enriched by the disproportioned chime of sin. Milton himself admits that there is beautiful music in hell, which from his account must be very like Wagner.

Such a concession to literary symbolism is a special rhetorical effect in music, a quite legitimate one, and a very ancient one. Plato's ideas of music are connected with it, and some later historical developments are studied in Mr. Hollander's paper. A once-famous poem called "The Lost Chord" depicts an organist discovering and then losing a wonderful chord which "seemed the harmonious echo To our discordant life," yet which musically speaking must have been a highly complicated discord, otherwise the sufferer could have found it again easily enough. This poem perfectly illustrates the confusion between the musical and the euphonious in literary criticism, as well as the persistent literary notion, found even in Browning's line quoted above, that music is concerned primarily with beauty of sound, especially as exemplified by concords. This is like saying that pictures are concerned primarily with pretty colors, especially the unmodified colors squeezed directly out of the tube. Music, of course, is concerned not with beauty of sound but with organization of sound, and beauty has to do with the form of the organization. A musical discord is not an unpleasant sound; it is a sound which throws the ear forward to the next beat: it is a sign of musical energy, not of musical incompetence. Applying such a principle to poetry, we should say that when we find sharp barking accents, long cumulative rhythms sweeping lines into paragraphs, crabbed and obscure language, mouthfuls of consonants, the spluttering rumble of long words, and the bite and grip of heavily stressed monosyllables, we are most likely to be reading a poet who is being influenced by music. Influenced, that is, by the music that we know, with its dance rhythm, discordant texture, and stress accent. The same principle suggests that the other use of the term "musical" to mean a careful balancing of vowels and a dreamy sensuous flow of sound actually applies to poetry that is unmusical, that is, which shows no influence from the art of music. Here is a passage from Tennyson's *Oenone:*

> O mother Ida, many-fountain'd Ida,
> Dear mother Ida, harken ere I die.
> I waited underneath the dawning hills,
> Aloft the mountain lawn was dewy-dark,
> And dewy dark aloft the mountain pine:
> Beautiful Paris, evil-hearted Paris,
> Leading a jet-black goat white-horn'd, white-hooved,
> Came up from reedy Simois all alone.

And here is a passage from Browning's *The Flight of the Duchess:*

> I could favour you with sundry touches
> Of the paint-smutches with which the Duchess
> Heightened the mellowness of her cheek's yellowness
> (To get on faster) until at last her
> Cheek grew to be one master-plaster
> Of mucus and fucus from mere use of ceruse:
> In short, she grew from scalp to udder
> Just the object to make you shudder.

Tennyson has tried to minimize the sense of movement, and it is hardly possible to read him too slowly; Browning has a stress accent, and goes at something like a metronome beat. Both passages repeat sounds very obtrusively, but the repetitions in Tennyson slow down the advance of ideas and narrative, compel the rhythm to return on itself, and elaborate what is essentially a pattern of varied and contrasting sound. The repetitions in Browning are intended to sharpen the accentuation of the beat and to increase the speed. Browning does not want a sound-pattern; he wants a cumulative rhythm. The words that Browning puts in parentheses ("To get on faster") are essentially a musical direction. Such musical directions are rare in poetry, but they do occur: the *mezzo-forte* direction for *Lycidas,* "Begin, and somewhat loudly sweep the string," is an example. Browning, therefore, is a musical poet, as his interest in music and in writing poems on musical subjects naturally suggest that he would be. Tennyson's poem is unmusical, which of course is not a pejorative term: it is unmusical for the same reason that it is a poor example of prose: it belongs to a different category. We should not be surprised to find what in fact is often true—that great unmusical poets develop a compensating interest in poetic opsis or visual imagery.

The chief characteristics of musical poetry are continuity and stress accent. Simple alliteration, as we have it in *Beowulf,* is musical in tendency; involved patterns of alliteration, as we have them in *The Faerie Queene,* are not. Run-on lines, and rhymes that sharpen the accent, like the rhymes in Browning, are musical; the rhythm and rhyme that tend to make the single line a unit in itself are unmusical. We notice that two of our most musical poets, Campion and Milton, opposed rhyme, at least in theory; and Milton's remark, in the Preface to *Paradise Lost,* that one of the features of "true musical delight" in poetry is "the sense variously drawn out from one verse into another," is one of the few technically accurate uses of the term musical in literary criticism. As we can see in such musical poems as Browning's *Heretic's Tragedy* or Burns's *Jolly Beggars,* musical verse is well adapted for the grotesque and the horrible; it is also eminently suitable for invective and abuse, for tangled and elliptical processes of thought, and for light verse of all kinds, from nursery rhymes to doggerel histories. In longer musical poems, such as Crashaw's hymns or Smart's *Song to David,* we often see passages of anaphora which resemble the sequential repetitions of music. In the emphatic use of thematic words, such as "life" and "death" at the beginning and the end of Crashaw's first St. Teresa ode, we may perhaps even see some analogy to musical tonality. Naturally the most difficult musical poems to identify as such are the slow movements, and the attempts of musical poets to give continuity to slow movement, such as the insistent beating short line in Browning's *Love among the Ruins,* have a particular technical interest. It is not surprising that many musical poets, like many composers, tend to get rather fidgety in a slow rhythm: Skelton is a good example.

Musical rhythm also has a natural affinity with poetic drama. Shakespeare's versification becomes steadily more musical as it goes on, this being the principle employed for dating his plays on internal evidence. The same distinctions apply equally to prose: if we are looking for musical prose, we should not turn to the mellifluous writers, to Jeremy Taylor or Walter Pater, but to Rabelais, Burton, Sterne, and, of course, James Joyce. The actual knowledge of music by musical writers is by no means invariable, nor should we expect it to be so: we should expect poets to learn techniques from their own art. But it is frequent enough to be statistically significant.

Many studies of the relation of music to poetry, such as Sidney Lanier's, are weakened by a tendency to base the relation on assonance and on ordinary metrical prosody. Most of our prosody consists of a translation into terms of stress of patterns that in their original Classical context were quantitative, and while

Classical poetry undoubtedly had close affinities with music, it was not the kind of music that poets of the last five centuries or so have been listening to. To read poetry which is musical in our sense we need a principle of accentual scansion, a regular recurrence of beats with a variable number of syllables between the beats. This corresponds to the general rhythm of the music in the Western tradition, where there is a regular stress accent with a variable number of notes in each measure. Musical poetry is considerably older than this kind of music, and the principle of accentual scansion is the dominant one in Old English poetry, where we have a four-beat line that seems to be inherent in the structure of the language, and continues in most nursery rhymes and ballads. The four-three-four-three quatrain of the ballads is actually a continuous four-beat rhythm, with a rest at the end of every other line. This principle of the rest, or the beat coming at a point of actual silence, was already established in Old English. All through the development of iambic pentameter, one can still hear, especially in blank verse, the old four-stress line in the accentuation:

> To *be,* or *not* to be, *that* is the *que*stion;
> *Whe*ther 'tis *nob*ler in the *mind* to *suf*fer
> The *slings* and *ar*rows of out*rage*ous *for*tune,
> Or *take* up *arms* against a *sea* of *trou*bles . . .

> Of *man's first* diso*bed*ience, and the *fruit*
> Of that for*bid*den *tree,* whose *mor*tal *taste*
> Brought *death* into the *world,* and *all* our *woe,*
> With *loss* of *Ed*en, till one *great*er *man*
> Re*store* us, and re*gain* the *blis*sful *seat* . . .

The general principle involved here is that when iambic pentameter is moving fairly fast, four-stress lines predominate. In the period of the stopped couplet the rhythm is slower and there are fewer four-stress lines, but they are still very frequent, and come back with any variation of the meter, such as a feminine caesura: "A *lit*tle *learn*ing is a *dan*gerous *thing* . . . ," or "Nor *hell* a *fury*, like a *wo*man *scorn'd* . . ." In Spenser and Keats there are still fewer, indicating that both poets belong to the tradition of unmusical opsis to which Tennyson also belongs. We notice in *The Faerie Queene,* for example, not only the recurrent Alexandrine but a number of six-stress pentameters: "The *build*er *oak, sole king* of *forests all* . . ." Also in *Lamia:* "Fair *Her*mes, *crown'd* with *feathers, flut*tering *light* . . ."

To have more than six accents is impracticable in a pentameter line except for some special rhetorical effect, as in the famous line in *Paradise Lost* (ii, 621) quoted by Mr. Oras, where there are eight. We notice that the slower the rhythm is, the more stressed monosyllables there are, and in so heavily stressed a language as English, the longer Latin words have the effect of lightening the rhythm by a series of unstressed syllables. The *reductio ad absurdum* of heavily stressed monosyllables is the horrible example in the *Essay on Criticism:* "When ten low words oft creep in one dull line." We note that poets in the opsis tradition tend increasingly to a strongly native vocabulary, where stressed monosyllables predominate: something of this comes into the fact that Keats found Milton so uncongenial an influence as compared with Spenser and Chatterton. In William Morris's *Earthly Paradise* there are many lines nearly as monosyllabic and motionless as the one Pope gives. On the other hand, almost any page of

Shakespeare will show what thunderous power a monosyllabic line may have in a more musical texture. Fewer than four stresses is also impracticable for a pentameter line. In most lines that look like three-stress lines, such as the second line of *Endymion*, we have usually to allow for rests—in this case there is one at the beginning of the line: "[*rest*] Its *love*liness in*crease*s: it will *neve*r . . ."

In Chaucer we have the curious example of an unmusical poet who has had an important musical influence. His basis is metrical rather than accentual scansion, but as the secret of his meter was lost he began to sound more like the accentual rim-ram-ruf poets he ridiculed, and that is the nature of his influence in *The Shepheards Calender* and elsewhere. Even before this happened, the confusion brought about by changes in pronunciation in the fifteenth century instantly re-established the four-stress accentual line. Lydgate, for instance, makes sense as a poet only when his alleged pentameters are read, not metrically, as we should read Chaucer, but accentually, with four main stresses to a line. One may not know the details of Lydgate's pronunciation, or precisely what syllables he would have elided or stressed differently, but possibly neither Lydgate nor his audience was entirely clear on such matters either, and a pattern of accentual rhythm is the obvious way of getting around such difficulties, as with accentual rhythm the number of syllables may vary within flexible limits.

The Scottish Chaucerians, as far as their rhythm is concerned, are Scottish Lydgatians. Dunbar is an intensely musical poet whose experiments often take the form of a kind of syncopated jazz or ragtime, for which English, with its heavy pounding accentuation, is so well adapted that even normally unmusical poets may be attracted to it. The ragtime tradition survives through Dryden's *Alexander's Feast* and Poe's *Raven* and *Bells* to Vachel Lindsay and *Sweeney Agonistes*. Syncopation is an unmistakable mark of musical poetry: Hopkins's sprung rhythm is a musical idea, whereas speeded-up metrical rhythms, such as Swinburne's roller-coaster anapests, are unmusical. An unmusical poet might conceivably have caught the movement of Browning's ride from Ghent to Aix, but only a musical poet could have been interested enough in the stumbling rhythm of a procession scrambling up a hillside to write the *Grammarian's Funeral*. In Skelton, who is so close to the popular rhythms of nursery rhyme, we still have predominantly a four-stress line, though in the opening of *Philip Sparowe,* a lively allegro march rhythm, there is an unusually large number of rests and accented beats coming together. It is clear in any case that when Coleridge announced with *Christabel* an entirely new principle of versification, a four-beat line with a variable number of syllables, the principle was about as new as such things generally are in literature. So far, I have observed very few departures from this four-beat common time in English: Mr. Eliot speaks of the rhythm of *The Cocktail Party* as a three-beat line, but I usually hear four beats, and so apparently do most of the actors.

Tudor tendencies, apart from drama, were mainly toward metrical regularity and away from musical influence, as we can see in Spenser, who begins with accentual experiments but abandons them later for an elaborate unmusical stanza. Spenser's development is the reverse of Milton's, who begins with stanzas and quickly turns to more continuous forms, notably the enjambed paragraph. The great dry recitativoes of *Samson Agonistes* are, as Hopkins said, perhaps our greatest achievement in musical poetry so far. Milton's chief musical contemporaries were Crashaw and Cowley. For most of his great religious poems Crashaw uses a free fantasia or ode form, which he often calls a hymn. The organization of these hymns is strongly musical, and they require a very fluent line which can lengthen or shorten at will, a pushing enjambement, and a fortissimo climax at the end. Cowley's Pindaric was evidently intended as a still freer development of the Crashaw hymn, in which rhythm and meaning could coincide.

The Augustan tradition again moved away from music, and Samuel Johnson's attitude to poetry is a consistently anti-musical one. In opposition to Milton's statement that in musical poetry the sense has to be variously drawn out from one line into another, Johnson says: "The musick of the English heroic line strikes the ear so faintly that it is easily lost, unless all the syllables of every line co-operate together: this co-operation can be obtained only by the preservation of every verse unmingled with another, as a distinct system of sounds." An abortive musical development began with Smart, Blake, and Burns—there are some fascinating comments on the musical resources of poetry in Smart's *Jubilate Agno*—but Romanticism was for the most part unmusical. On the other hand, if we have understood what musical poetry tries to do, we should have more sympathy with what Wordsworth, without any knowledge of music, was trying to do in *The Idiot Boy* and *Peter Bell,* and perhaps also with what Southey was trying to do in *Thalaba.*

Many post-*Christabel* experiments can be reduced to a four-beat accentual line. Meredith's *Love in the Valley* is based on such a line, very similar in its rhythm to much of Lydgate. The four-

stress line of *Hiawatha,* whatever its Finnish origin, fits English
very snugly, which perhaps explains why it is one of the easiest
poems in the language to parody. The general tendency of free
verse is unmusical. When rhythm is variable there is no point in
a run-on line, and we notice that in Whitman the end of each line
is marked by a strong pause, which means that Whitman's rhythm
has little in common with the continuous rhythm of music. Imag-
ism, as its name indicates, threw a strong emphasis on opsis, and
began an almost consciously anti-musical development. Eliot's
1936 essay on Milton, where he put Milton and Joyce, quite cor-
rectly, into the musical tradition and then surrounded that tradition with deprecatory value-judgements, is the culmination of
this movement. But even before this Eliot's growing interest in
drama had begun to convert him to a more musical point of view.
Pound, too, is a much more musical poet than the quality of his
influence would lead us to expect, and he has been able to absorb
at least two strongly musical influences, Browning and the Old
English alliterative line. The influence of Auden, whose *Oxford
Book of Light Verse* is full (it comes close to being an anthology)
of musical poetry, has also been thrown largely on the musical
side.

So far I have been speaking of melos as an influence on poetry
from music as we know it, music organized by stress accent and
dance rhythm. There is however another type of melos, and one
which more naturally comes to mind when we think of the musical element in literature. This is the melody and rhythm of lexis
itself, the melos produced by the rising and falling inflections and
the pattern of emphasis in the spoken word. More attention has

been paid to this than to the influence of music on poetry, but its study is badly handicapped by the fact that no satisfactory notation has yet been devised for it. When it comes to reproducing the melody and rhythm of speech, typography is helpless and the notation of ordinary music worse than useless, because, with its rigorous framework of an enharmonic scale and its equal divisions of time-values, it is actively misleading. The patterns of the voice traced by an oscillograph are much closer to what a proper notation would be.

When we listen to a reading of Dylan Thomas, say the reading of Peacock's *Song of Dinas Vawr,* which is in the Harvard collection, we are struck by the slowness of the reading. The words have it all their own way here: they organize the rhythm, and are not subordinated to a continuous stress beat. Next we are struck by the importance of two features which are traditional in poetry but have little place in music as such. One is an approximately regular pattern of pitch accent, which has been replaced by stress accent in music. The other is an emphasis on the varying sonority of vowels, which in Classical poetry would take the regular form of a quantitative meter. The equivalent of quantity in English might better be described as quality, the sense that some kind of irregular patterning of vowel-sounds is present.

These elements of pitch accent and quality of assonance are a part of chanting, and singing and chanting are, in modern times, radically different methods of associating melos and lexis. When a poem is set to music and sung, its rhythm is taken over by music. When it is chanted, all musical elements are subordinated to the words. We notice that poets who, like Yeats, want their poems chanted are precisely those who are most suspicious of musical settings. Thus the contrast between musical and unmusical poets partly resolves itself into a contrast between two conceptions of melos: one which reflects the external influence of the autonomous art of music, and one which incorporates certain musical elements into a verbal structure. Poe's *Poetic Principle,* for example, makes statements about the role of music in poetry which make up in strength what they lack in precision, but Poe is talking about the second kind of melos, the kind which has nothing directly to do with music, and usually produces unmusical poetry. Of such are the problems of criticism.

There are, of course, differences of degree in the absorption of words by music in musical settings. The madrigal, where the words are tossed about from voice to voice, represents an extreme limit in the subservience of poetry, and the dislike of poets for this trituration of their rhythm can be seen in the support they gave to the development of the seventeenth-century monodic forms. Henry Lawes went further than most composers of his day in approximating the rhythms of music and poetry, and so won the applause of Milton: "Thou honorest verse," Milton says. In the nineteenth century the admiration expressed by many symbolist writers for Wagner was in part based on the notion—if so erroneous a notion can be said to be a base—that Wagner was trying to give the literary elements equal prominence with the music. The modern convention in song-writing also prescribes close attention to the rhythm of the words. Nevertheless music remains music, and poetry poetry, each a world of its own. It is probable that Greek poetry and Greek music met together in a kind of no-man's-land of tonal magic in which musical and poetic elements were barely distinguishable. One can find something of the same thing as late as *Aucassin et Nicolette*. But ever since music became a fully autonomous art, this central area has disappeared, and in modern combinations of music and poetry one art regularly absorbs the other. That is why the two kinds of melos in poetry afford such a striking contrast in technique. There are tendencies today, ranging from the strong verbal emphasis in folk song to what is called *Sprechgesang,* which may modify this situation, but it still exists.

The chanting of verse tends to give it a hieratic quality, removing it from the language of common speech, and it thereby increases the exhilaration of poetry, bringing it nearer to the sphere of the heroic. In drama this stylizing of speech takes the form of declamation, which is also appropriate to heroic themes. Declamation is also a feature of rhetoric and oratory, where again we can see literary analogues of musical elements: oratory, for instance, resembles music and differs from ordinary speech in its use of patterns of repetition. How much oratory depends on melos can be realized if we walk along a residential street on Sunday morning listening to the radios in the houses. The words may not be audible, but one can generally distinguish, from the cadences alone, the sermon, the prayer, the commercial, and the newscast. This suggests that the sound-patterns of ordinary rhetoric are reducible to a few basic formulas, some of them nearly as invariable as the rise and fall that the sharp ear of Mark Twain caught in a clergyman's reading and recorded in *Tom Sawyer*.

The sound-patterns of poetry are of course very complex: a recent issue of the *Kenyon Review* has demonstrated how complex they can be. Ten competent readers of one poem will produce ten different but equally valid sound-patterns. It seems to me

that the only way to introduce order into such a subject is to begin
by distinguishing the different rhythms which form the basis of
reading. Let us take a line of poetry at random, say the opening
line of Claudio's great speech in *Measure for Measure:* "Ay, but
to die, and go we know not where." Here we have, in the first
place, the metrical or prosodic rhythm, an iambic pentameter with
the first foot reversed. Second, we have the accentual rhythm, in
this case a four-stress line. Third, we have the semantic or prose
rhythm, the rhythm of sense, which in this case corresponds very
closely to the accentual rhythm. Fourth, we have the mimetic
rhythm which results from the actor's attempt to catch the mode of
speech of a man in imminent fear of death. Mimetic rhythm is of
course most important in drama, but it is found in other genres too,
as a reader must at least imitate the mood of the piece he is reading.
Onomatopoeia is a by-product of mimetic rhythm. Fifth, we have
an oracular, meditative, soliloquizing rhythm emerging from the
coincidences of the sound-pattern, or what we have called the
quality of assonance:

> Ay;
> but to die . . .
> > > and go
> > > we know
> > > > not where.

This rhythm is not very prominent in drama, but in lyric, especially free verse lyrics in short lines, like the poems of Cummings,
it is one of the predominant rhythms. Each of these rhythms has
its own pattern of stress and pitch, and the particular blend of

them that any reader will make will depend on his sensitivity to some as compared with others.

The study of the complex sound-patterns of poetry has greatly lagged behind the study of the complex patterns of meaning, largely because of the lack of a notation already mentioned. The study of complex meaning, or ambiguity, has enriched our appreciation of poetry, and at the same time, in the form of semantics, it has helped us to see through the illegitimate use of ambiguity in rhetoric, the employing of weasel words with a strong emotional impact and a shifting meaning. Similarly, the study of the sound-patterns of poetry and drama would both increase our understanding of literature and help us to take a more clinical view of the hee-hawing of demagoguery, whether evangelical or political. In any case it would help to prevent poetry from becoming bogged down in books, and would do much to restore to it its primitive gift of charm.

PART ONE

Words into Music: The Composer's Approach
to the Text

"I AM SENDING YOU a few more of my compositions, and although, except for the *Ständchen,* there is nothing new among them, nevertheless none has appeared in print. They are almost all composed with respect for the meter and the verse-form, and I should like to prove myself worthy of my thorough instruction in this branch of the art. The short verses, among the long, are the most difficult to set to music, if one grants in addition that the tone and spirit of a poem should likewise not be neglected." [1] So wrote Zelter to Goethe in 1800, at the beginning of their long correspondence. And the composer's "respect for the meter and the verse-form" was rewarded by the poet's highest praise, for twenty years later Goethe wrote: "I feel that your compositions are, so to speak, identical with my songs; the music, like gas blown into a balloon, merely carries them into the heavens. With other composers, I must first observe how they have conceived my song, and what they have made of it." [2]

[1] Max Hecker, editor: *Der Briefwechsel zwischen Goethe und Zelter* (Insel-Verlag, Leipzig, 1913), I, 9. Translation my own.

[2] *Ibid.,* II, 59.

Today it is hard for us to understand Goethe's preference for Zelter's tuneful trifles over the masterpieces of Schubert, but we must remember that these men were facing a newly arisen problem—how to set to music a pre-existing poetic text not specifically written for this purpose. A short and necessarily very superficial glance over the history of text-setting may help to clarify the nature of the difficulty.

During the Renaissance, the forms of vocal music were to a great extent determined by the words, whether the latter were, in the case of secular song, poems written for this purpose, or, in sacred music, texts of Biblical or liturgical origin. Independent instrumental forms hardly existed before the seventeenth century, so that it was natural that the motivic shapes, the phrase-structure, and the overall articulation, of the music should be determined by the clearest form-giving element, namely the text. With the rise of modern tonality in the seventeenth century, however, abstract and completely independent musical forms evolved. The freely articulated music of the sixteenth century gradually gave way to tight, logical, self-sufficient structures. Except in the recitative, which, as a compromise between speech and song, remained tied fairly strictly to the verbal declamation, songs came more and more to be based on these abstract forms, and the texts had to be written accordingly. Thus the typical Metastasian aria was designed to be fitted to the *da capo* form; and its lines were short enough and simple enough to permit the composer to fill out his musical form with the word and phrase repetitions, the melismas, and the cadenzas, typical of the late Baroque Italian opera.

One result of the triumph of the musical over the poetic form was that most serious poets began to turn their attention elsewhere. The poet-musician of the Renaissance disappeared, and with few exceptions the major poets of the period gave little thought to the possibilities of musical setting. But toward the end of the eighteenth century composers began to look longingly in the direction of the great poets, and the poets themselves, inspired by the growing interest in folk song and balladry, thought once more of music. But the old days of verbal supremacy were gone forever: abstract tonal structure was now much too firm to yield to any externally imposed conditions. How then could poet and composer, each insisting on the validity of his own artistic pattern, come to terms with each other?

This is the problem for which Zelter was attempting to find a solution, and in a letter of January 10, 1824, he explains to Goethe his method of working: "Above all I respect the form of the poem and try to perceive my poet therein, since I imagine that he, in his capacity as poet, conceived a melody hovering before him. If I can enter into rapport with him, and divine his melody so well that he himself feels at home with it, then our melody will indeed be satisfying.

"That this melody should fit all strophes is a condition that is not clear even to the better composers. The objections against this are not unknown to me; you, dear friend, will at least realize at this point that I am not in favor of the *durchkomponiert* method of setting strophic poems. Others will hold otherwise, and may act accordingly; although a melody which one doesn't enjoy hearing several times is probably not the best." [3]

When we look at Zelter's songs, we find that he is as good as his word: the external form of the stanza is rigidly respected, and he

[3] *Ibid.,* II, 262.

builds his simple melodies to conform thereto—melodies which must therefore be repeated throughout, with only such variation as a good performance can accomplish. It is the easiest solution, but one which pleased Goethe, who, as a poet, preferred to see music in a secondary role and liked to think of the composer as merely uncovering the melody already concealed in his own word-rhythms. As for the emotional and pictorial possibilities of the music, he felt that they must be limited and subordinate. "The purest and highest painting in music is the kind that you practise: it is a question of transporting the listener into the mood indicated by the poem; then the imagination, without knowing how, sees forms taking shape in accordance with the text. You have produced models of this in *Johanna Sebus, Mitternacht, Über allen Gipfeln Ist Ruh,* and where indeed not? Show me who besides yourself has accomplished the like." [4]

Today we feel inclined to answer that although Schubert may not have accomplished the like, he produced something better still—a song that when necessary sacrificed the stanza-pattern for the sake of a higher dramatic or rhetorical unity, a song that was not content with vaguely indicating the mood of the poem but instead actively shaped its emotional content anew in accordance with its own interpretation.

A comparison of Schubert's setting of Goethe's familiar *Wanderers Nachtlied* ("Über allen Gipfeln Ist Ruh") with Zelter's, so highly praised in the passage just quoted, is instructive. [5] Zelter, keeping close to the unusual stanza-form (even though he has the

---

[4] *Ibid.,* II, 57. In this connection, see also Frederick W. Sternfeld: "The Musical Springs of Goethe's Poetry," in *The Musical Quarterly,* XXXV, 4, (October, 1949) pp. 511–25.

[5] A selection of Zelter's songs, including this one, is reprinted as one of the publications of the Paul Hirsch Music Library (Martin Breslauer,

temerity to repeat *balde* twice), produces a top-heavy musical period: it attempts to balance an antecedent of five and one-half measures with a consequent of only three and one-half. The conclusion thus arrives much too soon; and in spite of the composer's obvious effort to create the mood he has indicated as *still und nächtlich,* the final impression is one of uneasiness and dissatisfaction. Schubert, on the other hand, willing to repeat words, phrases, and entire lines, produces an almost diametrically opposite musical form: he balances an antecedent of four measures with a consequent of four and one-half and produces a further extension by repeating the final two and one-half measures. The musical design contradicts the stanza-pattern, but the connotations of *Warte nur, balde/ Ruhest du auch* are given vivid expression.

The objection would of course be raised by the Zelter school that Schubert achieves this result only through a violation of the poetic form. Such a conception of form is a very narrow one, however; form properly considered involves the organization of all the elements of a work of art and is by no means a matter of pure surface-pattern. Defined in this way, form must of necessity be multiple—ambiguous if you like—for it is impossible for an observer to see a work from all points of view at once. Architecture and sculpture furnish immediate examples, for it is obvious that buildings and statues present an infinity of visual forms, each corresponding to a different position of the beholder. *"The* form" of the building or statue is an abstraction, insofar as it can never actually be seen and can only be reconstructed mentally as the sum or resultant of the multiple visual forms.

A few examples from music will show the same principle at

Berlin, 1924). Another, edited by Ludwig Landshoft, was published by B. Schott's Söhne (Mainz, 1932).

work. Any single performance of a composition, no matter how conscientious, can at best present a limited view of the complex whole. The phrasing of a fugue-subject, for instance, must influence the shape of the entire piece; and there are few subjects for which one ideal phrasing can be found. In the Chromatic Fugue of Bach, one possible choice would be to emphasize the sequential pattern of the subject; another would be to bring out the descending structural line. The two interpretations, each valid yet to a certain extent contradicting the other, produce corresponding total musical forms in the fugue as a whole—and these are by no means the only possible ones. Nor is the multiplicity of form in a single composition limited to its varying performances. Rarely do all the form-giving elements exactly coincide, so that one can read a composition in many ways, depending on the relative weight one gives to melodic line, motivic structure, harmonic progression, and temporal proportions. If we hear the first movement of Mozart's C-major Piano Sonata (K. 545) primarily in thematic terms, we shall place the recapitulation at the return of the first theme; if we hear it tonally we shall say that the true recapitulation occurs only with the return of the second.

Like music, poetry exhibits different forms depending on the aspect the reader considers as most important. Verse-form and metrical structure are often at odds with syntactic logic: I need not enlarge on the run-on lines of late Shakespeare and the failure of the Miltonic sonnet to observe the octave-sestet division. The traditional ballad by its very nature confines a progressive narrative within a static and repetitive strophic pattern. And as in music, much is determined by the interpreter, the silent or vocal reader who must constantly make decisions about speed, emphasis, tone, accent, and inflection. Indeed, poetry is much less determinate than music in these respects and offers to the interpreter what a musician would consider a bewildering infinity of choices. Not only that: in reading or listening to poetry, the mind can move backwards and forwards through the work; it can subconsciously accept or reject many possibilities of meaning and interpretation; it is constantly busy making comparisons and clarifying relationships. In a word, it is constantly trying to apprehend the poem under many of its possible forms. Not so in music, where the mind is so to speak chained to the vehicle of the moving sound. If it tries to struggle free of the present moment, it finds that it has lost the music in so doing. Hence it must follow the piece through from beginning to end, and it must perforce be satisfied with those relationships immediately perceptible during the one journey. But if poetry is more flexible in this regard, music is more vivid; by the very concentration it requires it presents its single aspect with greater immediacy and with the illusion of closer personal contact.

What the composer does, then, when he sets a poem to music, is to choose one among all its forms—or, more accurately, since it is impossible, except by abstraction, to isolate one single form, he delimits one sub-set within the complete set of all possible forms. The one so chosen may previously have been obvious to every reader, or it may have been concealed to all except the composer. At any rate it might well be termed a latent form of the poem; and, if you will forgive the word-plays, I should say that the composer's task is to make the *latent* form *patent* by presenting it through the more specific, inflexible, and immediate medium of music. Since he is, after all, primarily a man of music, his choice will be determined not only by his conception of the poem but also by his recognition of the potentialities of realizing this conception in a valid musical structure. I do not wish to discuss here the difficult question of the extent to which the presence of a text can make up for deficiencies in purely musical logic, but it is clear from the works themselves that the great song-composers of the romantic and modern periods insisted upon musical construction that was self-sufficient, although not necessarily definable in terms of abstract instrumental patterns.

The familiar example of Schubert's setting of *Der Erlkönig* will show at a glance what I mean. Once he had made the decision to renounce the simple quatrains of Goethe's ballad in favor of a *durchkomponiert* design following the climactic narrative, he had still to find a way of producing a satisfactory musical unity. This he did by means of the constantly reiterated accompaniment figures, and by the translation of the child's successive outcries into three exactly parallel but tonally progressive climaxes.

It is not always so easy. Matthias Claudius' poem *Der Tod und das Mädchen* presented a real problem in its unmediated contrast between the maiden's wild expostulation and Death's soothing reply. Schubert prevented his setting from falling into two unrelated sections by allowing the piano to precede the entrance of the voice, stating at the outset the theme to be used later by Death in his response. Thus the musical design, in contradistinction to the poetic one, is the familiar three-part ABA pattern. But note that Schubert, in balancing his purely musical form, at the same time clarified the dramatic structure of the poem. It is obvious that the text plunges *in medias res,* that Death has already

appeared to the maiden before she speaks, and it is this situation
that Schubert has made clear by his introduction. I could not wish
for a more beautiful example of latent form translated into
patent, and it is quite possible that Schubert had this purpose in
mind rather than the strictly musical one when he composed the
introduction. It makes no difference; the two results go hand in
hand.

Sometimes in his attempt to create a satisfactory musical shape
the composer resorts to a device which should apparently be con-
demned by anyone sensitive to poetic values: he forces the text
into an arbitrary mold by the repetition of words and phrases.
I grant that the motivation for so doing is usually non-poetic,
but I believe that a justification can be argued in poetic terms;
at any rate I think that the practice does less harm to the text than
is generally assumed. If in reading poetry our consciousness (or
perhaps better our subconsciousness) hovers over certain words,
and ranges both forward in anticipation and backward in memory, an actual phonographic recording of our thoughts would
probably involve a great deal of repetition not unlike that made
explicit in certain songs. Here again is Schubert's version of
Goethe's *Wanderers Nachtlied,* the repetitions all being Schubert's
own:

> Über allen Gipfeln
> Ist Ruh,
> In allen Wipfeln
> Spürest du
> Kaum einen Hauch;
> Die Vöglein schweigen, schweigen im Walde.
> Warte nur, warte nur, balde

Ruhest du auch;
Warte nur, warte nur, balde
Ruhest du auch.

Is this an insensitive reading of the original? I can well imagine
a reader pausing on *schweigen* to savor the image of the birds
(the only form of animal life evoked in the poem). The suggestion of holding back implicit in *Warte nur* might cause him to
dwell for a moment longer on that phrase; and lastly, on finish-
ing the poem, he might prolong its effect by rereading the final
lines.

To test this theory I have applied it to one of the extreme examples of the literature: Schumann's version of Heine's *Ich
grolle nicht*. Here are the original lyric and Schumann's version,
which not only repeats arbitrarily but departs sharply from the
correct stanza division:

Heine: Ich grolle nicht, und wenn das Herz auch bricht,
            Ewig verlor'nes Lieb, ich grolle nicht.
            Wie du auch strahlst in Diamantenpracht,
            Es fällt kein Strahl in deines Herzens nacht.

            Das weiss ich längst. Ich sah dich ja im Traume
            Und sah die Nacht in deines Herzens Raume,
            Und sah die Schlang', die dir am Herzen frisst,
            Ich sah, mein Lieb, wie sehr du elend bist.

Schumann: Ich grolle nicht, und wenn das Herz auch bricht,
            Ewig verlor'nes Lieb,
            Ewig verlor'nes Lieb, ich grolle nicht,
                        ich grolle nicht.

Wie du auch strahlst in Diamantenpracht,
Es fällt kein Strahl in deines Herzens Nacht,
Das weiss ich längst.

Ich grolle nicht, und wenn das Herz auch bricht,
Ich sah dich ja im Traume,
Und sah die Nacht in deines Herzens Raume,
Und sah die Schlang', die dir am Herzen frisst,
Ich sah, mein Lieb, wie sehr du elend bist.
Ich grolle nicht,
Ich grolle nicht.

The repetitions in the first stanza seem to me quite natural and explicable along the lines indicated in the preceding example. The linking of *Das weiss ich längst* with the first stanza is more dubious; yet logically *Das* refers backward rather than forward, and Schumann has certainly made this clear. It is still harder to justify the return to the opening lines immediately afterward, although it is easy to see that Schumann badly needed them for reasons of thematic parallelism. But another motivation was perhaps suggested by Heine himself when he returned to *Ich grolle nicht* at the end of his own second line. These words become, as it were, an *ostinato* motif, heard by implication underneath everything that follows, the purpose of which after all is to explain why the protagonist is not angry even though his heart is breaking. Schumann has made this *ostinato* explicit, and has chosen logical places to do so: after the pause suggested by the connotations of *längst* (a pause lengthened by the musical setting), and at the very end, when the listener's thoughts would naturally return to the initial paradox.

This explanation may not be convincing and I do not insist upon it, but I do insist that it is too facile to claim that every such repetition and rearrangement is an arbitrary violation of the poetic design.

Faults in prosody constitute another difficulty for critics who disagree with Mahler's reputed statement that a good song is of necessity a badly declaimed one. If Mahler actually said this, he was merely pointing out by exaggeration that musical prosody can never be a slavish imitation of verbal accentuation, for although musical and verbal meters are in many respects analogous, they by no means exactly coincide. Moreover, we tend to forget to what extent prosody is a matter of convention. *La donna é mobile* is rendered by Verdi with a strong accent on *la*—a license consecrated by centuries of tradition in Italian. In English we should not tolerate a similar accent on *the,* but we allow an analogous distortion in Purcell's "Whén I am laid in earth."

Some so-called errors of this kind are errors of performance rather than of composition. Failure to recognize Handel's hemioles leads to such absurdities as "The glory of the Lord shall be ré-veal-ed." But even outright mistakes such as Berlioz's *offerímus* at most distort the sound of the word and leave the sense clear. What of accentuation that, by its falsification of values, alters the meaning of a passage by throwing the emphasis on the wrong word? We must be careful here, for the composer by so doing may be revealing to us an interpretation we had not previously considered. To those who have always read, "And God said, let there be light: and there *was* light," Haydn's version "and there was *light"* must come as a shock; yet no one can hear

Haydn's setting without admitting its fundamental correctness—
a correctness supported incidentally by the original Hebrew.

A less familiar example is Hindemith's "La Belle Dame sans
Merci," where Keats's fourth line is rendered: "And no birds
sing." On the face of it this is a bad mistake, perhaps occasioned
by Hindemith's inadequate command of English. Further consideration might lead to the conclusion that Hindemith's knowledge of the language is on the contrary a subtle one and that he
has chosen this way of emphasizing that not even the birds sing
on this bleak hillside. In a narrow sense, Hindemith's setting is
probably not correct, for it violates the prevailing metrical pattern; but it is interesting because it suggests a new way of inter-
preting the line.

If I have said little about content as such in the foregoing discussion of the problems of text-setting it is because I believe what
I hope has already become obvious: that content and form are
inseparable, and that we cannot speak about the one without implying the other. The concept of musical content is so moot that
I prefer to base my arguments on the fairly concrete grounds of
form, but if a musical setting is able to vitalize and vivify one
among the many aspects of the total form of a poem, by so doing
it presents a unique interpretation of the poem's meaning. Otherwise it would necessarily detract from our comprehension of the
words, for by emphasizing purely sensuous enjoyment on the one
hand or emotional stimulation on the other it would draw our
attention away from the text. Ultimately there can be only one
justification for the serious composition of a song: it must be an
attempt to increase our understanding of the poem.

FREDERICK W. STERNFELD

Poetry and Music—Joyce's Ulysses

THE IMPORTANCE OF MUSIC for poetry has been the subject of many rhapsodic discourses, yet the precise manner in which the art of tones may influence the art of words has remained both fascinating and obscure. I should like to approach this elusive topic on three levels: the setting of new texts to old tunes; the transfer of modes of expression from a musical to a verbal organization; and the function of a musical composition as analogue or symbol for a work of literature.

I. WANDERING MELODIES

The first of these to consider are the "wandering melodies," that is to say, the tunes that hover in a poet's ear before he feels impelled to create a new text to an old song. There may exist a mood, an atmosphere that is impatient for expression, but its crystallization into verbal form has not taken place. Not until the poet hears a tune, one that is exactly right, its lilt and sing-song the inevitable carrier for what needs saying, does the poem take definite shape. The melody which brings it to life has "wandered" from its old text and its past associations into a new context to which it conveys not only its properties of rhythm and pitch but also some aspects of its original mood and content. Inevitably, the new creation is haunted by elements of the poetic model: it may be a single word or, more likely, a phrase—sometimes an entire refrain, a feeling, an emotion, a passion; a landscape (or seascape) against which the poem is set; a thought or an action.

"Action" is a hallowed term which recalls Aristotle's definition of poetry as the imitation of an action. Properly understood, this comprehensive term subsumes all the elements of content—verbal, emotional, intellectual, dramatic, which may singly or together wander from poem to poem, carried by a certain tune. A Platonist would probably say "idea," where the Aristotelian speaks of action, but whatever the term it must be remembered that our poet not only recreates life, he also recreates another poem.

"Tell me the songs to which you sing, and I shall tell you what poet you are," one may paraphrase, meaning not how good a poet but what kind of poet. For the models of the wandering melodies give us pregnant clues to the emotional and mental climate out of which a poem is born and to the kind of poetry which most deeply affects the poet at this stage of his development. Marlowe's tuneful "Come live with me and be my love" has been the inspiration of many a poet, including Raleigh, Herrick, and Donne. Raleigh's famous reply is contemporary, as is Shakespeare's quotation of the second stanza in *The Merry Wives:* "To shallow rivers to whose falls/ Melodious birds sing madrigals" (III,1,16). But, to focus on twentieth-century Dublin, Cecil Day Lewis, by means of a significant variation, evokes the stress and strain of the current social malaise: "At evening by the sour canals/ We'll hope to hear some madrigals." The fact that the wandering melody is well known helps in establishing the irony of Lewis' parody. Unhappily, a writer cannot assume that his readers are familiar with the tune he has in mind, and a prose poet has a further difficulty in that his audience is less homogeneous than, say, Shakespeare's was, and less restricted than that of a lyrical poet such as Yeats or Lewis. Joyce circumvents the difficulty at times by inserting musical notation in the midst of his letter press, a practice not unlike the rubric of the ballad operas, "to the tune of . . ." (Consider, for example, the Ballad of Persse O'Reilly in *Finnegans Wake*, p. 44.) At other times his cues may be cryptic, for who would attempt to deny that Joyce was fond of riddles? Such passages must be read aloud, with sensitivity, and the solution will come.

When Stephen Dedalus challenges two of the librarians in the National Library of Dublin (calling them by the actual names of two of its incumbents early in the century), the discussion wanders along in prose, interspersed with an occasional stanza, until, with subtle shifts of tone and association Goethe's Wilhelm Meister and Dumas, *père et fils,* lead to the father/son aspect of Hamlet and Shakespeare: "Explain you then. Explain the swansong too wherein he has recommended her to posterity." (p. 200) Eglinton's reply is typographically set to resemble verse:

> You mean the will.
> That has been explained, I believe, by jurists.
> She was entitled to her widow's dower
> At common law . . .

Stephen mocks:

> And therefore he left out her name
> From the first draft but he did not leave out
> The presents for his granddaughter, for his daughters,

> For his sister, for his old cronies at Stratford
> And in London. And therefore when he was urged,
> As I believe, to name her,
> He left her his
> Secondbest
> Bed.

> *Punkt*

> Leftherhis
> Secondbest
> Bestabed
> Secabest
> Leftabed.
> Woa!

The lines are printed as verse, but the speakers' diction does not observe this. Eglinton's line, "That has been explained, I believe, by jurists" has an exceedingly prosaic ring. Stephen's language is, understandably, more poetic, but still encumbered by pedestrian phrases, such as, "As I believe," Only as the lines grow shorter

> He left her his
> Secondbest
> Bed

does the verse division force upon us a declamation tending toward poetry.

What were the associations floating about in Joyce's mind as he wrote this episode? The cryptic rubric *Punkt* offers a clue. First, and unmistakably, we have reached a pause, the reader is to take a breath, to resume with a new intonation. Second, the model of this new intonation is probably German. This scrambled

speech is brought up short with "Woa!" Typographically set to
the left, it completes the tune on which the preceding word play
is modeled:

Example 1

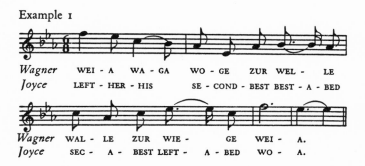

To an habitué of the opera in Dublin, London, or Paris, the
song of the Rhine maidens was an old familiar; and in the poetry
of the 1920s Wagner's melodies were no newcomers. Eliot had
quoted Kurwenal's song in *The Waste Land,* and had also utilized
Wagner's four-stress lines in a reference to the Rhine-daughters
as a counterpart of the Thames-daughters. Isolde's "Mild und
leise" distorted into "meldundleize" (*Finnegans Wake,* p. 18) is
only another reminder of the erudition which the writers in the
Joyce-Pound-Eliot group assume on the part of their readers. But
their familiarity with the German composer's works did not always induce admiration for them, and Wagner's tetralogy was
not a favorite. "Wagnerian music, though confessedly grand in
its way, was a bit too heavy for Bloom and hard to follow . . ."
(*Ulysses,* p. 645). Joyce takes obvious delight in poking fun at its
hymnic solemnity, for there is irony in the stuffy rubric *Punkt;*
at the same time he utilizes Wagner's melody to heighten the

poetic recitation to actual song. Nor can Joyce resist a passing barb at Librarian Best: "It is clear that there were two beds, a best and a secondbest, Mr. Secondbest Best said finely."

The antecedents of a poem can often be precisely documented in the correspondence between poet and fellow-poet or merely friend. Yeats's *Three Bushes* deserves notice in this respect, as it made its appearance in the mid-thirties at a time when Yeats, in his late life, was desperately striving to recapture for poetry the social and convivial pleasure it had enjoyed in the time of Burns. Yeats made this deliberate attempt to bring together again the long separated sister arts while he was editor of *Broadsides,* published by the Cuala Press in Dublin in the years 1935 and 1937. Each song was accompanied by its tune in musical notation and several musicians in Dublin and London acted as arrangers or composers. There were "songs by new poets, set in the traditional way," as the preface states. Yeats might have said, texts to old tunes, and one of them, in particular, had an interesting history. Dorothy Wellesley's "The Lady, the Squire and the Serving Maid" bore the rubric, "Tune, 'The Brisk Young Bachelor' from 'A Collection of Old English Songs' by Cecil Sharp." The attraction this folk-song had obviously lay in its rhythmical properties which were so suitable for Dorothy Wellesley's ballad. Beyond this, the unabashed frankness with which the folk text regarded sex struck a sympathetic note both for Wellesley and Yeats in this year, 1935. To the tune of "The Brisk Young Bachelor" Wellesley then wrote five stanzas, reciting the tale of the lady who bid her servant maid take her place in her lover's bed. Yeats apparently took spontaneous delight in the content and sing-song of this new poem and wrote, "When I got your first sketch I went down stairs humming over the opening stanzas, getting the rhymes regular . . ."[1] He could, of course, see ways of refinement and proceeded to write a version of his own, related in content. As his title, "The Three Bushes" implies, the poetic symbol of the rosebush which, at the last, unites the separate graves of the lovers, had a special fascination for him. Yeats's poem followed the same form as the original of six-line stanzas, alternating lines of four and three stresses. He continued revising until it seemed to him just right, being careful, however, that it would go "with your music," for he felt that the two poems belonged together. When Wellesley finally consented to "the regular rhymes," she wrote: "If you should ever print it for the Cuala [Press] please use it with the tune I sent, found for me by Mrs. Gordon Woodhouse: 'The brisk young bachelor,' which is printed in Cecil Sharp's 2nd volume of *English Folk Songs* (Selected Edition, Novello & Co.) No. 25, page 60, from Somerset"—a more accurate rubric than that published by the Cuala Press. (See Example 2.)

In 1937 the *Broadsides* printed Yeats's "Come gather round me Parnellites," fitted, appropriately enough, to a traditional Irish melody. The poem is as nationalistic as it is occasional, in the truest sense of the word, since it was written for the Dublin of Yeats's own time. Singing, not silent reading, is demanded of this lyric which its author deliberately chose to open this edition of the *Broadsides*. My reason for mentioning this song is its frank

---

[1] Cf. *Letters on Poetry from W. B. Yeats to Dorothy Wellesley* (London, 1940), W[ellesley] p. 77, Y[eats] p. 79, W 80, Y 81, Y 82, Y 83, Y 87, W 88, Y 89, Y 104, Y 114, W 142. There is a good deal of further correspondence and revising (W 142, Y 142, W 144, Y 145, Y 152, W 161, Y 162, Y 163, Y 166) for the process of adapting wandering melodies tends to be continuous.

Example 2

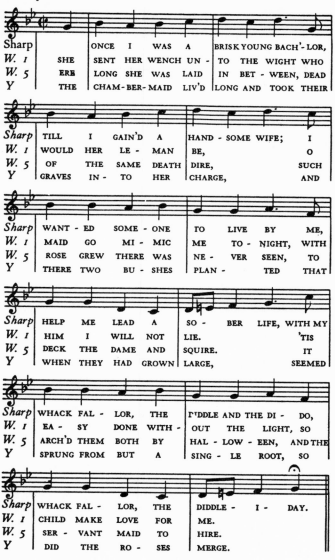

conviviality. In his preface to the *Broadsides* Yeats stresses the fact that he is not thinking of the concert platform but of a group of friends gathered in a public house. Goethe, in his Almanac of 1804 (*Taschenbuch auf das Jahr 1804*) had a similar notion. Of the scores of wandering melodies which served Goethe's muse a very considerable proportion was intended for convivial singing.

Conviviality erases the bleak anonymity that mostly separates an author from his mass audience and fosters a personal relationship between the two. Hence, in *Ulysses* some of the most effective uses of music are set in an atmosphere of conviviality. "Bob Cowley's twinkling fingers in the treble played again. . . . *Light*-ly he *played* a *light bright tink*-ling *mea*-sure for *trip*-ping *la*-dies, *arch* and *smil*-ing *and* for their *gal*-lants, *gen*-tlemen *friends*." (p. 277) The light bright tune imposes its rhythm on the hearer. (Italics above indicate stressed syllables.)

The minuet from Mozart's *Don Giovanni*, a backdrop for Bloom's tragedy, creeps by degrees into the rhythm and singsong of Bloom's thought as he sits in the Ormond bar. By the time we reach the next sentence accents are not enough, the actual melody is needed:

Example 3

ONE: ONE, ONE, ONE: TWO,   ONE, THREE, FOUR

This is followed by the conscious recognition of the tune which Bloom had been humming subconsciously only a moment before and the music then conjures up in his mind a mise-en-scène: "Minuet of Don Giovanni he's playing now. Court dresses of all descriptions in castle chambers dancing. Misery. Peasants outside. Green starving faces eating dockleaves." Quickly his aural perception pulls him back to the melody and with the four monosyllables that follow his thoughts again sway with the minuet: "Nice that is. Look:"

Example 4

LOOK, LOOK, LOOK, LOOK, LOOK: YOU LOOK AT US

"That's joyful I can feel. Never have written it. Why? My joy is other joy. But both are joys. Yes, joy it must be. Mere fact of music shows you are."

Don Giovanni gives way to the "Croppy Boy," which Ben Dollard renders in the words of Carroll Malone to the tune of an old Irish melody that has not ceased to wander since it was first registered in London in 1582. "Callin o custure me" [2] has an engaging history and with slight deviations in its spelling has been variously and frequently referred to in Elizabethan and Jacobean literature. Shakespeare, Dekker, Nashe, and Davies have all mentioned it, and musical versions of one melody survive in manuscripts at Cambridge and Dublin while Playford's *Musical Companion* contains a slightly different tune but with the same Irish title. [3] Playford's Irish text runs: "Callino callino callino castore

[2] A Transcript of the Registers of the Company of Stationers of London, ed. E. Arber, 5 vols. (1875–1894), II, 407. The first English text appeared in 1584.

[3] Cambridge University Library, Ms. Dd. 4.23. f. 19 (transcribed later in this essay in Example 5); Fitzwilliam Museum, Cambridge University,

me/ Eva ee eva ee loo loo loo lee." The meaning of these Irish
words is shadowy, to say the least, and it is not surprising that the
tune was regarded by English readers as distinctly (and fiercely)
Irish, indeed, alien. The ebullient Pistol in *Henry V,* IV, iv, declares "Calin o custure me" to be unintelligible gibberish, and
John Davies of Hereford, in the *Scourge of Folly* (Epigram 73)
sums up the reaction of those who speak English but not Irish:

> But it was like the burden of a song
> Call'd "Calino," come from a foreign land
> Which English people do not understand.

The English text of 1584 is but one of many verses which the
wandering melody supports, as the following examples show:

Anonymous, 1584:   When *as* I *view* your *com*-ly *grace*
                              Ca-len   *o*   cus-*tu*-re *me* . . .

Malone, 1845:   Good *men* and *true!* in this *house* who *dwell,*
                              To a *stran*-ger bou-*chàl* I *pray* you *tell* . . .

Graves, 1882:   *When* I *march*-ed a-*way* to *war,*
                              How you *kiss*'d me *o'er* and *o'er,* . . .

---

the famous ms. known as the "Fitzwilliam Virginal Book," p. 277 of
the ms., and Vol. II, p. 186 of the transcription by J. A. Fuller-Maitland
and W. Barclay Squire, 2 vols. (Leipzig, 1894–1899); Trinity College
Library, Dublin, Ms. D. 1. 21, known as "William Ballet's Lute Book,"
p. 85 of ms., and transcribed by Donal O'Sullivan in *Grove's Dictionary
of Music* . . . 5th ed. (London, 1955), III, pp. 289–99, s. v. "Folk Music:
Irish"; John Playford, *Catch that catch can, or the Musical Companion,*
(London, 1667), p. 231.

Hyde, 1895:   *Hap*-py *this* thou *blind,* for *thee,*
                     That thou *see*'st not *our star,* . . .[4]

The tune must have been fairly prevalent after 1845, since Duffy's *Ballad Poetry of Ireland* alone appeared in over forty editions, and the mere titles of the Stanford and Graves collections would assure wide distribution. But, the origin and meaning of the song, obscure for hundreds of years, had, in fact, aroused no perceptible curiosity until, in 1790, Edmund Malone (educated at Trinity College, Dublin) brought out his edition of Shakespeare's plays. In his commentary he traces the song to its Irish origin, though he erroneously derived the words "Calin o custure" from "coleen ogh a stor," meaning "young girl, my darling." Succeeding editors accepted Malone's commentary, apparently without further question, and no satisfactory explanation of the original text appeared until 1939, near the end of Joyce's life. At that time Gerard Murphy proffered a modern scholarly explanation.[5]

Such academic minutiae probably mattered little to Carroll Malone (*nom de plume* of William B. McBurney, said to have been a doctor in Northern Ireland before he emigrated to America where he was an early contributor to *The Nation*) when he wrote "The Croppy Boy," to celebrate the Irish rebellion of 1798, gave it the caption of "A Ballad of '98," and wedded it to the

[4] *1584:* Clement Robinson's poetic miscellany, *Handful of Pleasant Delights,* ed. Hyder E. Rollins, 1924, p. 38; *1845:* C. G. Duffy, *Ballad Poetry of Ireland,* 3d ed. (Dublin, 1845) p. 156; *1882:* C. V. Stanford, *Songs of Old Ireland* (London, Boosey [preface 1882]), p. 21; *1895:* A. P. Graves, *Irish Song Book,* 2d ed. (London, Dublin, New York, 1895), p. 170.

[5] "Callen o custure me," in *Eigse: A Journal of Irish Studies* (Dublin, 1939–40), I, 127–29.

rousing Irish air of "Calino" with its distinctive Irish lilt and rhythm.[6] The tune was exactly apt for Carroll Malone's patriotic Irish poem, and that its curious title was even then a mystery to the natives of Dublin or Belfast mattered not.

Back in the Ormond Bar one of the men has asked for more Mozart, oddly enough for the lofty aria of Sarastro in the *Magic Flute,* "qui sdegno non s'accende" ("In diesen heil'gen Hallen"). "No, Ben, *The Croppy Boy.* Our Native Doric," is the counter-suggestion, and the song of the Irish insurrection carries the day. Bloom feels impelled to go, yet cannot make himself, and in the following four pages, interspersed with Bloom's thoughts, we hear "The Croppy Boy," sung in a low voice, to the traditional Elizabethan melody. "Chordsdark. Lugugugubrious. Low. In a cave of the dark middle earth . . ." And "The voice of warning, of solemn warning . . . told them how solemn fell his foot-step . . ." As "Ben Dollard's voice barreltone" drones on, the "voice of penance and of grief," we hear the song almost in its entirety, though the text is distorted, depending on the impact of certain phrases on Bloom's mind—a mind that reacts by selection and reverberation.

> At the siege of Ross did my father fall,
> And at Gorey my loving brothers all,

[6] There are, actually, two ballads entitled "The Croppy Boy," different in tune as well as in text, but both dealing with the Wexford rebels of 1798: the ballad by Carroll Malone, sung to the tune, "Callino," as used by James Joyce and given in Example 5; and the folk ballad beginning either " 'Twas early, early, all in the spring" or " 'Twas very early in the spring," printed in P. W. Joyce, *Ancient Irish Music* (Dublin, 1873), p. 62, and in W. B. Yeats' *Broadside* (Dublin, Cuala Press), October, 1935.

> I alone am left of my name and race,
> I will go to Wexford and take their place. (stanza 5)

To troubled, introspective Bloom whose only son, Rudy, was dead, these lines are strangely and "solemnly" moving. Joyce amplifies the resonance of the crucial words:

> All gone, all fallen. At the siege of Ross his father, at Gorey all his brothers fell. . . . Last of his name and race.
> I, too, last my race. . . . Well my fault, perhaps. No son. Rudy. Too late now. Or if not? If not? If still?
> . . . Rudy. Soon I am old . . .
> . . . Bloom, soon old but when was young. (p. 280)

In this manner many individual words and phrases are actually quoted, yet disfigured, and transfigured perhaps, through Bloom's depression.

Ben Dollard's "sighing voice of sorrow" intones verse after verse. The sixth stanza of the ballad:

> I cursed three times since last Easter day—
> At masstime once I went to play;
> I passed the churchyard one day in haste,
> And forgot to pray for my mother's rest,

is paraphrased (*Ulysses,* p. 279): "Since easter he had cursed three times. You bitch's bast. And once at masstime he had gone to play. Once by the churchyard he had passed and for his mother's rest he had not prayed. A boy. A croppy boy." The allusion is clearly to Stephen Dedalus, as the reverberation of these lines, 300 pages later in the novel, shows. Like Joyce himself, he had

refused to make his peace both with his mother and with organized religion, even at his dying mother's behest. Typographically
set up like a work for the stage, Joyce depicts Stephen's hallucina-
tions in the brothel scene (p. 578):

THE CROPPY BOY

Horhot ho hray ho rhothers hest
(*He gives up the ghost* . . .)

In this scene there is only one other quotation from "The
Croppy Boy," slightly parodied, but in metred lines.

Ballad, stanza 7:

I bear no hate against living thing;
But I love my country above the king.
Now, Father! bless me and let me go
To die, if God has ordained it so.

Ormond scene (p. 280):

He bore no hate.
Hate, love . . .
Big Ben his voice unfolded . . .
Ireland comes now. My country above the king . . .
Bless me, father [Joyce's italics]. Dollard the croppy cried.
Bless me and let me go.

Tap.
Bloom looked, unblessed to go . . .
Low sank the music, air and words . . .

Brothel scene (p. 578):

THE CROPPY BOY

(*The rope noose round his neck* . . .)
I bear no hate to a living thing,
But love my country beyond the king.

The Ormond scene includes the important phrase "Father, bless me and let me go," in italics for emphasis, since it focuses on Stephen's desperate search for a true father and on Bloom's eagerness to be such a father to Dedalus. Yet, the lines in the brothel scene are more easily singable, since the presentation is dramatic. The more reflective Ormond scene, on the other hand, reproduces the song by indirection and refraction. In example 5, the upper staff gives the sixteenth-century song, "Callino" or "Calen o" from Cambridge University Library Ms. Dd. 4.23.[7] The ms. contains thirty-five leaves of music, and f. 19 has "Callino Robinson," that is "Callino" as arranged for cittern by Thomas Robinson. The transcription has been made by the present author, and the text is from *A Handful of Pleasant Delights,* 1584, edited by H. E. Rollins (1924), p. 38. The lower staff gives one of the many arrangements of "Callino," this one from the *Popular Album of Irish Songs,* edited and arranged Hubert Rooney, (Dublin & London, n.d.), pp. 12–13. Rooney gives Carroll Malone as the author of the text and cites as the source of his music: "Air: Cailin og a Stor." Below Malone's text are added Joyce's modifications of it.

There is a sardonic humor in these Joycean distortions, the

---

[7] Cf. *A Catalogue of the Manuscripts Preserved in the Library of the University of Cambridge,* 5 vols. (Cambridge, 1856–67), I, 228.

Example 5

Elizabethan WHEN AS I VIEW YOUR COME - LY GRACE,

Malone 6 I | CURSED THREE TIMES SINCE LAST | EA - STER DAY, AT
Malone 7 I | BEAR NO HATE A - GAINST | LI - VING THING, BUT I
Joyce I | BEAR NO HATE TO A | LI - VING THING, BUT

Elizabethan CA - LEN O CUS - TU - RE ME, YOUR GOL-DEN HAIRS, YOUR

Malone 6 MASS - TIME ONCE I | WENT TO PLAY, I
Malone 7 LOVE MY COUNTRY A - | BOVE MY KING, NOW
Joyce LOVE MY COUNTRY BEY - | OND THE KING

Malone 6 PASS'D THE CHURCH - YARD ONE
Malone 7 FA - THER BLESS ME AND

Elizabethan AN - GEL'S FACE, CA - LEN O CUS - TU - RE ME.

Malone 6 DAY IN HASTE AND FOR | - GOT TO PRAY FOR MY | MO-THER'S REST,
Joyce HOR - | HOT HO HRAY HO | RHO-THERS HEST
Malone 7 LET ME GO TO | DIE IF GOD HAS OR - | DAIN'D IT SO.

"Woa" instead of Wagner's "Weia," the counterpointing of the comic aspects of the brothel setting and Stephen Dedalus's physical discomfort set against the inner struggle of his conscience which causes him to take on the role of the "croppy boy" and to sing "horhot ho hray" (forgot to pray). This kind of travesty has played an important role in the history of "wandering melodies," so much so that the original Greek "par-odia," meaning "to an ode, to a melody," became transmuted to the current literary meaning of "parody." But when the "croppy boy" in *Ulysses* sings that he loves his country "beyond the king," instead of "above my king" as in Malone's ballad, Joyce has simply re-created the phrase as it reverberated in his auditory memory, with no concern for scholarly exactitude. Again, Bloom, depressed and apathetic, ruminates,

> Hamlet, I am thy father's spirit
> Doomed for a certain time to walk the earth (p. 150)

at this moment himself walking the daytime earth, not "the night," as Shakespeare has it. Also, the commercial traveler of Dublin is more likely to speak of a "certain time" than of a "certain term," as does his royal model. Such creative adaptations are part and parcel of the oral tradition, as the poet works through the ear. His concern is for the right tone for his wandering melody, rather than accuracy of reproduction.

In the context of *Ulysses* the minuet from *Don Giovanni* and the Dublin ballad do not function merely as pleasant or doleful melodies: they highlight the significance of the scenes which they counterpoint. The overtones of plot and archetype which Joyce derives from Mozart's opera for his analysis of Bloom and Dedalus will be discussed in the third portion of this essay, and the implications of the "croppy boy" in regard to the search for a father and the break with mother and religion have just been touched upon. Similarly, C. D. Lewis uses an Arcadian song as an ironical foil, and Wellesley and the old Yeats avail themselves of a folk-song—with its frankness and earthiness—to achieve the directness and concreteness they desire. The drinking melodies used by Goethe in his *Taschenbuch* and Yeats in his *Broadsides* are not only easy to sing, they stand for a milieu which the oral poet finds so sadly lacking in his bookish, urban environment. Regrettably, modern authors may not always count on their readers' knowledge of the models which they put to such trenchant use. Shakespeare's audience—they were primarily auditors, not readers!—knew the text of the "Willow Song" and responded unhesitatingly to the changes which the poet wrought on the original. But in the case of Yeats, Lewis, and Joyce modern scholarship must sometimes perform an interpreter's function. Be that as it may, when the proper melody for a poetic passage comes to light, we discover more than mere music. We find a means to prove the poet's mind, his likes and dislikes, the social milieu he hopes for, and his deep-seated fears.

II. MUSICAL ORGANIZATION

An awareness on the part of the poet of the procedures of music constitutes another sphere of influence that music may exercise on poetry. Obviously, it is not the direct influence of a certain tune or rhythm, but the subtle application of musical practices to poetic creation. Such a transfer from an art made of tones to one of words presupposes a familiarity on the poet's part with

standard musical techniques, though in the case of wandering
melodies it is frequently possible almost mechanically to syn-
chronize a new text with an old tune. But, in its superb examples
the synchronization is far from slavish (italics indicate stress):

> Vaux: I *loathe* that *I* did *love*
> Shakespeare: In *youth* when *I* did love
> Vaux: In *youth* that *I* thought *sweet*
> Shakespeare: Me-*thought* it was *ve*-ry *sweet*
> Vaux: As *time*   re-   *quires* for *my* be-*hove*
> Shakespeare: To *con*-tract oh the *time* for a- *my* be-*hove*
> Vaux: Me- *thinks*   they   *are* not *meet*
> Shakespeare: O me- *thought* there a-was *no*-thing a- *meet*

There are four extra syllables in Shakespeare's last two lines,
for the purpose of vocalization (or exclamation): "contract oh,"
"for a," "there a," "nothing a." Of these all four appear in the
"good" quarto of 1604/05, and the first two in the Folio of 1623,
and, as Clark and Wright have pointed out, represent the drawl-
ing notes in which the clown sings—like "stile-a" and "mile-a"
in Autolycus' song in *Winter's Tale*, IV, ii. And here we have
one of the important instances of music's penetrating influence,
namely, the on-rush of syllables, the sense of motion and even
hurry, by which one is propelled from one stressed syllable to
the next. Yeats, discussing the poetry of Gerard Manley Hopkins,
properly dwelt on "this stoppage and sudden on-rush of syllables"
as "a necessary expression of his slight, constant excitement."

Other characteristics that mark the influence of musical procedures are lines of greatly uneven length and a prominent and
extensive use of monosyllables. Here again the analogy is obvious.

For in music a unit of time, say a four-bar phrase, may be taken up with four whole notes (or semi-breves) as easily as with a proliferation of stressed and unstressed notes. Ben Jonson, that favorite author of Joyce (particularly in the younger years when Joyce's "mind turned often for its pleasure to the dainty songs of the Elizabethans") supplies an apt example in his poem from *Cynthia's Revels:*

> Slow, slow, fresh fount, keep time with my salt tears;
>   Yet slower yet; O faintly, gentle springs;
>   List to the heavy part the music bears,
>   Woe weeps out her division when she sings.
>   Droop herbs and flow'rs
>   Fall grief in show'rs
>   Our beauties are not ours;
>   O, I could still
>   Like melting snow upon some craggy hill
>   Drop, drop, drop, drop
>   Since nature's pride is now a withered daffodil.

Beginning with a line of ten syllables and ending with twelve, the stanza is interspersed with several shorter lines (5-8) which prepare for the famous penultimate line. With only four mono-syllables, this line is yet long and full.[8]

The reference to Joyce's fondness for Elizabethan song occurs in his *Portrait of the Artist as a Young Man*. He has Stephen Dedalus "repeat the song by Ben Jonson which begins: 'I was not

---

[8] For a more detailed analysis of this poem, cf. C. Ing, *Elizabethan Lyrics* (London, 1951), p. 121 ff. *et passim;* also my comments on Ing's approach in terming lines 1 and 10 "isochronous," *Shakespeare Quarterly,* IV (1953), 79-83.

wearier where I lay . . .'" In *Ulysses* (p. 645 f.) "Stephen . . .
launched out into praises of Shakespeare's songs, at least of in
or about that period, the lutenist Dowland . . . and Farnaby and
son with their *dux* and *comes* conceits and Byrd (William),
who played the virginals . . . and one Tomkins who made toys
or airs and John Bull." One can only conclude from this comprehensive array that Joyce must have been familiar with the
Fitzwilliam Virginal Book.

The technique of lines of uneven length is so inherent in
musical composition that it is a characteristic of all madrigal and
lutenist verse. Dowland's famous "Weep you no more sad foun-
tains" ends its stanza, after eight lines of seven, six or five syllables,
with one of only two syllables, the single word, "sleeping." Similar
Elizabethan musical rhythms occur in *Ulysses:*

> And in London. And therefore when he was urged,
> As I believe, to name her,
> He left her his
> Secondbest
> Bed.

This radical reduction of eleven syllables to one is not of itself
music, but it is an application of the organization of music to
verbal organization.

The use of repetition in poetic creation is still another exercise
of musical procedure—repetition that frequently does not make
sense but that does make superb sound. The penultimate line
from Ben Jonson's "Slow, slow, fresh fount" is a good example
of the cumulative impact of the fourfold repetition of a mono-
syllable: "Drop, drop, drop, drop" gathers momentum as it

moves along, in striking contrast to merely rhetorical repetition which is essentially motionless, as Tennyson's *"Break, break, break/* On thy *cold* gray *stones, O Sea."* But Joyce's "Look: look, look, look, look, look, you look at us" moves forward.

The distinction between visual poetry which functions in the manner of "a cinema in which images flash across a stationary background" and musical poetry, "A vehicle which collects images in the course of its own movement" has been ably set forth by Northrop Frye in an article entitled "Music in Poetry":

> When we find . . . a dreamy sensuous flow of language, we are probably dealing with an unmusical poet. When we find sharp, barking accents, crabbed and obscure language . . . the bite and grip of many monosyllables, we are probably dealing with a musician.
>
> Certain corollaries follow. The musical, or cacophonous, diction is better fitted for the grotesque and horrible. . . . It demands a long, cumulative rhythm sweeping up the lines into larger rhythmic units such as the paragraph . . .
>
> Of course, musical poetry is likely to relapse into doggerel or prosiness in the attempt to fill out these larger rhythms, but it is congenial to a gnarled intellectualism of the so-called "metaphysical" type. It goes without saying that it is irregular in metre, leans heavily on enjambement, and makes an important feature of syncopation, in poetry the clash between metrical and semantic rhythms. This syncopation is a sure mark of musical poetry and helps in distinguishing it from speeded-up unmusical verse. Hopkins' sprung rhythm is, in origin, a musical idea . . .

This last apt reference is reminiscent of Yeats's comment (*Oxford Book of Modern Verse*, p. xxxix) that sprung verse "enables the poet to employ words taken over from science or the newspaper without stressing the more unmusical syllables," an astute assessment by a poet on the other side of the fence. An illustration from Hopkins's *Leaden Echo* combines the stress on the more musical syllables, the onrush over the unmusical, "the bite and grip of many monosyllables," and the almost excessive employment of repetition: "How to keép—is there ány any, is there none such, no—[pause] where/ known some, bow or brooch or braid or brace, lâce, latch/ or catch or key to keep/ Back beauty, keep it, beauty, beauty, beaúty . . ."

The pause between the two syllables of "no-where" has been inserted for the purposes of this essay. The primary stresses on "keep" in the first line and "beauty" in the fourth line; the secondary stress on "any" in the first, and the fermata (hold) on "lace" in the second line, occur all in Hopkins' own ms.[9] Also note that twenty-four monosyllables intervene before the main phrase, "to keep back beauty" is completed.

Consider now the poem with which Joyce completes his early volume *Chamber Music* (1907); "I hear an army charging."

I moan in sleep when I hear afar their whirling laughter.
They cleave the gloom of dreams, a blinding flame,
Clanging, clanging upon the heart as upon an anvil.

.   .   .   .

They come out of the sea and run shouting by the shore.

[9] Cf. W. H. Gardner's chapter, "The New Rhythm" in his *Hopkins*, 2 vols (London, 1944–49), particularly II, 106.

My heart, have you no wisdom thus to despair?
My love, my love, my love, why have you left me alone?

(ll. 6–12)

The twofold repetition of "clanging" in line 8 prepares for the threefold repetition of "my love" in line 12. This is the last line of the poem and of the book; its emphasis is deliberate and made the more solemn by the syncopation of the following syllable "why." Keeping in mind Frye's definition of syncopation, "the clash between metrical and semantic rhythms," we express the intensity of the question by *"why* have you left me a-*lone?"* The metrically irregular accent on "why," following immediately upon the accented "love" (an accent made prominent by its three-fold statement) enforces the kind of pause between "love" and "why" that is an ear-mark of musical poetry, as is the on-rush of syllables between "why" and "[a]-lone" in the second half of the line. The ultimate syllable "lone" is made emphatic by the alliteration which connects it with "love," "love," "love," "left." The phrase "hear afar" in line 6 is one of Joyce's favorites and is symptomatic of his auditory sensitivity which perceives even distant and faint sonorities. Such phrases as "bronze from anear by gold from afar, heard . . . anear . . . afar" and "hearing the plash of waves . . . anear, afar, they listened" occur again and again in *Ulysses* in another section of the Ormond Bar chapter. Three concatenations of monosyllables begin lines 6, 7, and 10 and thus prepare for the climax of the ultimate line, an uninterrupted procession of eleven monosyllables before the final "a-lone."

The climax of the final line is achieved by a number of means: the clash of stresses on "why," the rhythm that springs from "why" to "-lone" and the exclusively monosyllabic structure, prepared by lines 6, 7, and 10. Thus, the verbal repetition of "my love" coincides with the reiteration of the rhythmic pattern of uninterrupted monosyllables, and this coincidence, to my way of thinking, is the best of the poem. In Joyce's prose as well there is plentiful repetition with its characteristic sweep, not only in short, monosyllabic passages, such as occur in several examples quoted earlier as wandering melodies (e.g., the *Don Giovanni* passage cited on page 24 and 25), but also the more complex, though no less musical repetition of "He left her his /Second-best/ Bed" (quoted on page 19).

Yeats's observation concerning Hopkins that this musical organization of verbal rhythm that is so irregular, so "sprung" "enables a poet to employ words taken over from science or the newspaper" can also be substantiated in *Ulysses*. Whether Joyce spends some pages giving us a scientific exposition of the properties of water, or whether, with the accuracy of an antiquarian and the irony of a poet, he chronicles in the minutest detail all the happenings reported in the Dublin newspapers for Blooms-day 1904, the Everyday of Everyman, as prosy, as journalistic, as humdrum as can be, he strains to the utmost the capacity of paragraphed prose, yet never abandons the principles of organization of musical poetry:

What in water did Bloom, waterlover, drawer of water, watercarrier . . . admire?
Its universality: its democratic equality and constancy to its nature in seeking its own level . . . its capacity to dis-*solve* and hold in *solution* all *soluble* substances . . . its meta-

morphoses as vapour, mist, cloud, rain, sleet, snow, hail . . .
[p. 655. Note, once again, the monosyllables. Italics added.]

But, of course, the climax of this technique, from the point of view of musical poetry, occurs in the chapter that narrates the events in the Hotel Ormond bar. There Joyce gives us a verbal reflection of the world of sounds, of the music of nature, of the clang of horses' hoofs, and the roar of the waves of the ocean, playing variations upon certain words and their sound: "ear, near, a-near, a-far, hear, hearing, heard" as the two barmaids, Miss Douce and Miss Kennedy listen both to horses' hoofs and the murmurs of the sea in a seashell. The very first line of the chapter announces the musical motif: "Bronze by gold heard the hoofirons steelyringing." This motif is then developed, sometimes more prosaically, "Bronze by gold, Miss Douce's head by Miss Kennedy's head, over the cross-blind of the Ormond bar heard the vice-regal hoofs go by, ringing steel." Sometimes more musically: "Yes, bronze from anear, by gold from afar, heard steel from anear, hoofs ring from afar, and heard steel-hoofs ringhoof ringsteel."

More and more the auditory perceptions permeate all other images until they overwhelm Bloom's mind before he leaves the Ormond Hotel. First, the music of the sea, as Lydia Douce, the barmaid, and George Lidwell are observed by him:

> To the end of the bar to him she bore lightly the spiked and winding seahorn that he, George Lidwell, solicitor, might hear.
> —Listen! she bade him . . .
> Ah, now he heard, she holding it to his ear. Hear! He heard. Wonderful. She held it to her own . . . To hear . . .

Bloom through the bardoor saw a shell held at their ears.
He heard more faintly that that they heard . . . hearing the
plash of waves, loudly, a silent roar.
Bronze by a weary gold, anear, afar, they listened. . . .
The sea they think they hear. Singing. A roar. The blood
it is. Souse in the ear sometimes. Well, it's a sea. Corpuscle
islands.
Wonderful really. So distinct. Again. George Lidwell held
its murmur, hearing . . . [p. 276]

There ensues then one of the many intertwinings between the
music of nature and the music of man, so characteristic of this
chapter. In it Bloom's thoughts actually sway unconsciously to
the melody from *Don Giovanni,* only to wander back to the
music of the seashell:

Sea, wind, leaves, thunder, waters, cows lowing, the cattle
market, cocks, (hens don't crow,) snake hissss. There's music
everywhere. Ruttledge's door; ee creaking (No that's noise.)
Minuet of *Don Giovanni* he is playing now. [p. 277. Parentheses added.]

As we have earlier remarked, Bloom's ruminative catalogue of
the music of nature ends with his conscious recognition of the
actual melody to which he has been listening. But, again, the
catalogue itself is musical poetry with its sudden and dramatic
change in voice register, in loudness and in tempo. The usual
typographical marks on the printed page such as parentheses,
dashes, and a variety of other punctuations, are indicated in music
by such rubrics as "tutti" vs. "concertino," "forte" vs. "piano
subito," "rallentando" vs. "a tempo."
The rationalistic strictures in Joyce's catalogue of nature's music,

"hens don't crow," "No, that's noise," the prosaic aside, "As I believe," in the National Library scene, one and all suggest the kind of voice-changes which a trained musician might observe as he follows the performance marks. This device is a further help in enabling the poet to "spring" from one sonorous phrase to the next and to sweep into the paragraph (or the stanza) a whole rush of unmusical, prosy syllables.

III. A WORK OF MUSIC AS ANALOGUE

There remains the symbolic importance of a work of music for a work of poetry. "Words? Music? No, it's what's behind" is Joyce's sensitive observation (*Ulysses*, p. 270). It explains his choice of *Don Giovanni*, along with the *Odyssey* and *Hamlet*, as his model for *Ulysses*. Undoubtedly there were many aspects of the opera that attracted Joyce over and above the tunes it yielded to the storehouse of his wandering melodies. (There are at least two other songs from the opera, not mentioned previously, that loom large in *Ulysses*—one is the duet between Don Giovanni and Zerlina, "La ci darem la mano," and the other is the Commander's "Don Giovanni, a cenar teco.") To be sure, these melodies were important building stones in the total edifice of the novel, but the ultimate significance of the opera lies deeper and on various levels. The obvious one to be observed at a first reading is the plot of *Don Giovanni*.

Bloom and his rival Boylan enter the Ormond bar at the same time but Boylan leaves shortly (whilst Bloom stays on) to rehearse "La ci darem la mano" with Bloom's wife. That Molly is betraying him Bloom knows, and from his many references to "La ci darem" we glean that he fancies himself in the role of Masetto to Boylan's Don. But as he lingers in the Hotel Ormond, composing an amorous letter to Martha Clifford, Bloom becomes Don Giovanni. This tormented hero is, in fact, full of fancy, and in an earlier episode (p. 177) his imagination embraces the Commander:

> He hummed, prolonging in solemn echo the closes of the bars:
>> Don Giovanni, a cenar teco
>> M'invitasti.
> —A cenar teco.
> What does that *teco* mean? Tonight perhaps.
>> Don Giovanni, thou hast me invited
>> To come to supper tonight,
>> The rum the rumdum.
> Doesn't go properly.

One could go on. Bloom is also Ottavio, the rightful betrothed, the careful and cautious man who loses the girl. But to restrict attention to these partial coincidences between the happenings in Dublin, Seville, Homer's Mediterranean, and Elsinore would be unfair to Joyce. For him the plot is not all-important, though it would be difficult to name which aspect is. Day-dream and night-dream unmask states of mind, pollution of mind, and catharsis. Words are molten and emerge in new shapes and sounds, revealing the mind's subtleties. Music is chanted, as background and foreground, expressing what words cannot and should not say. There is the mind of the author himself, of which we are constantly aware. We hear the characters of the novel through his inner ear in which fragments of his countless models sound, providing counterpoint to Bloomsday and giving a depth to the happenings in Dublin that removes them from the parochial.

When Bloom muses, on his way to Davy Byrne's (p. 150):

That is how poets write, the similar sounds. But then Shakespeare has no rhymes: blank verse. The flow of language
it is. The thoughts. Solemn.

> Hamlet, I am thy father's spirit
> Doomed for a certain time to walk the earth.

the quotation shows an eddy of Bloom's stream of consciousness,
more important, it brings to light the paradigm in Joyce's mind
for the father-son fable in modern times. Deliberately he sums up
Shakespeare's unrhymed blank verse as "solemn" and carefully
terms as "solemn" the echo with which Bloom prolongs the
cadences of "Don Giovanni a cenar teco." The overtones of this
attribute sound in the "solemn music" of Shakespeare's last plays,
"that Shakespeherian Rag," as Eliot has it in *The Waste Land*.[10]
The *Don Giovanni* fragment refers not only to Bloom's desire
to avenge, it serves to emphasize the continuity of the poetic
myth from Homer to Shakespeare, to Mozart and to the creator

---

[10] The disposition of the words "solemn," "solemnly," "solemnity"
throughout *Ulysses* is indicative of Joyce's general care in the choice of his
vocabulary. Miles Hanley, in his *Word Index to Ulysses*, lists 25 occurences,
and the majority of them are strategically placed in the novel. Quite often
they are part of the stage directions which indicate a mock Mass or a Black
Mass. There the use of the term on the first page of *Ulysses*, when Buck
Mulligan (alias Gogarty) intones the ritual of the shaving bowl, is significant (p. 5; cf. also p. 24). And seven more passages occur in the Black
Mass of the brothel scene. The Shakespeare chapter in the National Library
is framed between a librarian's dignity and Mulligan's mock-masque, and
here again Joyce's employment of the epithet "solemn" is both ritualistic
and ironical. Together with the passages concerned with the re-telling of
the "Croppy Boy," and allusions to Shakespeare and Don Giovanni (or
Don Juan) we have 16 of the 25 listings. The remainder are fairly obvious
in their direct or indirect reference to liturgical or clerical dignity, court
ceremony, or Irish nationalism.

of Stephen Dedalus. The "solemn" cadences, the terrifying, bare octave leaps of the Commander's eerie arrival (in D minor) endow the wanderings of Bloom with a tragic depth ". . . the fundamental and the dominant are separated by the greatest possible interval . . . The ultimate return. The octave." That primary interval, the octave, which conveys such symbolic meaning in Mozart, comes in for some of Stephen's musings in the brothel scene (p. 494), underlining once more the correspondence of fables that are separated in time but, in their togetherness, constitute the poetic whole: "God, the sun, Shakespeare, a commercial traveller having itself traversed in reality itself, becomes that self." The symbolic interpretation of musical intervals has a long tradition in Western civilization, proceeding from Pythagoras to the early church fathers, on to scholasticism and the Renaissance. With Joyce's Jesuitical training, it is not surprising that his knowledge of music embraced ancient and scholastic philosophy in addition to his native discernment and experience as a singer. The ultimate return of the octave symbolizes the ultimate return of God in Everyman, the commercial traveler of Dublin, the "usylessly" Ulysses.

For the final shape of the novel, however, Joyce's training and proficiency as an Irish tenor are not to be dismissed lightly. Here a comparison of his use of the famous octave leaps with that in Shaw's *Man and Superman* is most enlightening. Shaw refers to instruments, specifically to the trombones which color the passage so uniquely, both in the overture that anticipates the scene, and in the finale when the statue of the Commander sings, "Don Giovanni, a cenar teco." Joyce's reference, on the other hand, is exclusively vocal, utilizing the Italian text and vocalizing "the

rum the rumdum." There is a fine significance in the fact that
Joyce should choose for his model an opera that conveys its
message through the human voice, abjuring that favorite ac-
cordion of the nineteenth century, the symphony orchestra. As
we have already seen, Wagner's operas were well known to him
from his youth, but the fact that they were scored for symphony
orchestra with voice obbligato was alien to the Irish Joyce's love
of cantabile. In Wagnerian opera, the essence of what the composer has to say, his over-all philosophy, and the unraveling
of his plot, are given to the orchestra, for it was Wagner's opinion
that this medium was ideal for communicating his artistic message.
His operas are the logical descendants of Beethoven's symphonies
and of German symphonies generally, in contrast to the Italianate
operas of Mozart and Gluck. This contrast was one cause of
Nietzsche's famous rejection of Wagner, a circumstance that
Joyce makes use of in his *Dubliners,* where James Duffy, whose
"liking for Mozart's music brought him sometimes to an opera
or a concert: these were the only dissipations of his life," we are
told, was a man on whose "shelves stood two volumes by Nietzsche, *Thus Spake Zarathustra* and *The Gay Science"* (pp. 135–39).
In the light of such a gospel—of a gay science, gay living (with
a twinkle of Irish humour), the long-winded, serious orchestral
operas of Wagner are either caricatured or dismissed in *Ulysses.*
When Stephen sings, with a smile, "to the air of the blood-oath
in the *Dusk of the Gods*

> Hangende Hunger,
> Fragende Frau,
> Macht uns alle kaput, (p. 547)

the final "kaput" is as satirical as "Woa" was in the *Rhinegold*
passage. And when, as Frank Budgen recounts, Joyce exclaims
at a concert in Zurich, "Listen, how full of grace and invention
is Mozart after the muscle-bound Beethoven," he merely articu-
lates Bloom's implied aesthetics. For the commercial traveler
from Dublin, having avowed that Wagnerian music was a bit
too heavy for his palate, goes on to enumerate his favorite cantabile
composers. "On the whole, though favoring preferably light
opera of the *Don Giovanni* description, and *Martha,* a gem in its
line, he had a *penchant* . . . for the severe classical school such
as Mendelssohn" (*Ulysses,* p. 645). *Mutatis mutandis,* this might
have been written by Wagner's most notorious critic, Eduard
Hanslick!

Don Giovanni has still another distinguishing characteristic
that is important for *Ulysses,* that its hero is a bass—a departure
from the accepted eighteenth-century pattern. The tenor voice, both
by the dearth of its occurrence and the frailty which so often goes
with it, is ill fitted for the role of prominence which the public today expects of it. In the realistic eighteenth century the hero was
either a castrato, that is, a singer who combined the lung power of
the male with the high range of the female, as in Gluck's *Orfeo,*
or he was a bass-baritone as in Mozart's *Figaro* and *Don Giovanni.*
With the advent of Romanticism there evolved the standard
cast of today, with the hero as a tenor and the heroine a soprano.
Mind you, the symbol of the strong hero and successful lover
fades noticeably when the role is cast in the tenor part, for the
belief that the bass is strong and the tenor weak and that the
strong man gets the girl is widespread in spite of the traditional

casting of nineteenth-century opera. The tenor hero is often doomed to be the prey of a destructive female: Aida clearly demolishes Radames and Carmen Don José. Reflections of this role are even to be found in Stravinsky's *Petrouchka,* where the successful Moor and his brawn are depicted in low-pitched instruments while the anguish of the unsuccessful Pierrot is given in the high-pitched cries of the trumpet. Joyce's choice of *Don Giovanni,* therefore, as one of the analogues of *Ulysses* signifies a sad tale: just as, throughout the opera the baritone Don Giovanni checks and foils his weak opponent, the tenor Ottavio, so the frail, sensitive, indecisive man is bound to lose. And this symbolism applies by no means only to Bloom, for it signifies even more acutely the plight of the poet-artist, of Stephen Dedalus. In this respect *Don Giovanni* is related to *Hamlet,* the other great analogue of *Ulysses.*

There is still another aspect in which Joyce's novel draws both on Mozart's opera and on Shakespeare's play; that is, the nexus of a family relationship. A younger generation, with its artistic ideals, breaks with the beliefs and customs of its elders; the son-artist rebels against the father. This is clearly the meaning of the National Library episode which offers the key to the problem of Joyce-Dedalus and which continues the intellectual autobiography, begun in *The Portrait of the Artist as a Young Man.* In keeping with Joyce's policy of indirection and refraction the subject is alluded to now and again with a seeming carelessness which bespeaks both the importance of the topic and the cunning of the author. ("Cunning indeed!" Cranly replies to Dedalus in the *Portrait,* "You poor poet, you!" when Dedalus confesses that he shall be "using for my defence the only arms I allow myself to use, silence, exile and cunning.") Dumas *père et fils* leads to Hamlet *père et fils* (p. 210):

—And what a character is Iago! undaunted John Eglinton exclaimed. When all is said Dumas *fils* (or is it Dumas *père?*) is right. After God Shakespeare has created most.

—Man delights him not nor woman neither, Stephen said. He returns after a life of absence to that spot of earth where he was born, where he has always been, man and boy, a silent witness and there, his journey of life ended, he plants his mulberry-tree in the earth. Then dies. The motion is ended. Grave-diggers bury Hamlet *père* and Hamlet *fils*. A king and a prince at last in death, with incidental music.

Wilhelm Meister, who fled from home and tradition, against the wishes of his father, to become an artist, opens this chapter ("And we have, have we not, those priceless pages of *Wilhelm Meister?*"); a chapter which continues the dialectical declaration of independence of Dedalus *fils* from the *Portrait*. For the poet's answer to Dedalus *père* (and even to Bloom, the quasi-*père*) shall always be *Non serviam*. Phrases like "the son consubstantial to the father" (p. 194) and Gregorian chants complete the analogy to Him who "there these nineteen hundred years sitteth on the right hand of His own Self but yet come in the latter day to doom the quick and dead when all the quick shall be dead already!" [Joyce now, page 195, proceeds to quote the chant *Gloria in excelsis Deo* in musical notation.] What then does Joyce mean when he speaks (p. 194) of Shakespeare's "assumed dongiovannism?" One must remember that the saga of Don Juan is not, primarily, that of a seducer, as it is sometimes popularly interpreted. Like the myth of Doctor Faustus, it depicts the rebellion of a Renaissance individual against scholastic tradition and dogma. Faustus wants knowledge at all costs; Don Juan wants love at all costs. Both are men of daring who think for themselves, unafraid of taboos. In Mozart's masterpiece, Don Giovanni rebels against tradition, personified in the father-figure of the Commander. His rebellion is uncompromising and final, as Kierkegaard has so properly pointed out in *Either/ Or*. When the Commander demands repentance, the Don's answer is a decisive "No." This refusal makes sense only on Kierkegaard's mythological level; it clearly is not motivated by sensual appetite, which would argue for life at all cost, even the shame of having betrayed one's artistic creed. Thus, Don Giovanni enters the chain: Stephen Dedalus-Wilhelm Meister-Hamlet-Shakespeare-Christ—a proud figure in a proud procession. The initial allusion to Wilhelm Meister, in itself the least important link, thus receives depth, for the intellectual core of Goethe's novel is a discussion of the Hamlet problem which is now rediscovered in the twentieth-century climate of Joyce.

The final aspect of *Don Giovanni* as an analogue for *Ulysses* goes beyond music, libretto, or even the archetype of its fable. It is involved with Mozart's aesthetics, the aesthetics which gave the old plot of Don Juan its immortal shape, Tirso de Molina, Molière, Byron, and Shaw notwithstanding. Why *Don Giovanni* is the perfect work of art is a question that has intrigued many a philosopher. Kierkegaard felt that music was the only proper means for expressing the subject matter, just as the Trojan War demanded the epic genre. I have tried in the preceding paragraphs to show how thoroughly congenial the *musical* fashioning of this myth must have been to Joyce. Still, this is not the crux of the matter as far as Joyce, the poet, is concerned. As an artificer, to quote his own designation, he was attracted by a quality that has been discussed in Schopenhauer's reminiscences. Plato's philosophy, Newton's optics, the perfection of Mozart—all were subjects of discussion with the aging Goethe, who had long been director of opera at Weimar. Why was *Don Giovanni* so incomparably great? asked the philosopher. Because, said Goethe, all is gay in the foreground, though Mozart never lets us forget the stark eternal tragedy of man hovering behind. Indeed, what unites *Don Giovanni* and *Hamlet* as types of artistic fashioning is that these works are not exclusively composed of tragic scenes, but that the comic scenes of Leporello and, say, the gravedigger, act as a foil to the stuff of which tragedy is made. The famous prophecy at the end of Plato's *Symposium* that neither the tragedian nor the comedian, but the tragi-comedian was destined to be the greatest poet has often been applied to Shakespeare. To which musical creations can this description point more aptly than the *opere buffe* of Mozart? The presence of laughter in Mozart's universe endows his art with humanity and makes it truly humanist, in the best Renaissance sense. For this reason his opera is bounded by Leporello's comic prologue at the beginning and the buffo-finale at the end. For *Don Giovanni* is not concluded in stark D minor, when the Commander's octave leaps, accompanied by funereal trombones, summon the hero to his death. The final peroration is the creed of the living, as the surviving characters articulate the story's moral and plan for the future—in the quick tempo of comedy, and in gay D major.

The affinity to *Ulysses,* which begins with the jokes of Buck Mulligan and ends with Molly Bloom's affirmation of life, is obvious. Less so, but equally important, is the relation between the artificer and his creation. For neither Joyce nor Mozart make their characters solely the mouthpieces of their own joys and fears, triumphs and frustrations. To be sure, their poetry is, and must be, a great confession as well. But they stand apart from their creatures, poised and controlled, content to speak through a dramatic context rather than in the first person. It has become fashionable to term this poise and moderation Apollinian, in contrast to Dionysiac art. I am not certain that the epithet Apollonian, which Nietzsche employs so happily in his *Birth of Tragedy out of the Spirit of Music* is an apt one for modern critics to use as a vignette for Joyce. It may have misleading overtones of idyllic serenity. Perhaps "ordered cosmos" gives a better intimation of the features which irresistibly drew Joyce to *Don Giovanni.* In terms of Greek philosophy "ordered" implies a musical organization, while "cosmos" points up the inclusion of laughter as well as the universality of the theme. And, finally, "ordered" also implies the deliberateness with which the theme is handled.

The twentieth century, which has so significantly rediscovered Mozart and re-evaluated the humor of Shakespeare, has reacted sharply against the aesthetics of the Victorians. We reject their modes of expression as too narrowly circumscribed, yet as too lushly exhibitionist. Both Shakespeare and Mozart have suggested a view of life that is wider and more controlled. That is why Joyce proudly painted on his banner both *Hamlet* and *Don Giovanni.*

Musica Mundana and Twelfth Night

"AS FOR the division," wrote Thomas Morley in the last decade of the sixteenth century, "music is either speculative or practical. Speculative is that kind of music which, by mathematical helps, seeketh the causes, properties and natures of sounds, by themselves and compared with others, proceeding no further, but content with the only contemplation of the art. Practical is that which teacheth all that may be known in songs, either for the understanding of other men's, or making of one's own . . ." [1] There is perhaps an echo of dispraise shown here by Morley, a most enterprising practical musician, for studies involving "the only contemplation of the art." But in his *Plain and Easy Introduction to Practical Music,* published in 1597, Morley could well choose to enforce such a distinction. His own century had inherited a rich tradition of discourse about music, both "speculative" and "practical," from the Middle Ages. It had produced a huge body of ad hoc theory occasioned by particular problems arising from contemporary musical customs.

[1] Thomas Morley, *A Plain and Easy Introduction to Practical Music,* ed. R. A. Harman (New York, 1953), p. 101.

Both of these and the growing Renaissance attention to the musical uses of antiquity combined in a tradition of encyclopedic musical learning. Such a monumental work was Gioseffe Zarlino's *Institutione Armoniche,* published in 1558, which devoted as much attention to such matters as classic myths of the power of music, general speculations of the nature of mathematical proportion, correspondences obtaining among tonal configurations, the elements and the humors, and so on, as it did to the exigencies of contrapuntal writing. The production of such compendia of lore, mistakes, natural science, aesthetics, and principles of craftsmanship was continued through the seventeenth century, as evidenced by the treatises of Robert Fludd, Mersenne, Praetorius, and Athanasius Kircher. Even before 1600, however, music as a subject for systematic writing embraced many different categories of thought and experience. At a time when musical practice had varied forms, each playing its respective social role and each generating its particular stylistic conventions, a simple description of "practical music" would be complex enough. But to this has to be added the strange body of theory and doctrine, mathematical, cosmological, prosodical, mythological, ethical, and pseudo-physiological that had accumulated during the Middle Ages. The Renaissance, with its increasing requirements by both amateur and professional musicians for practical investigation, was unable to dispense with such an accumulation of authority on the subject of music's *raison d'être.*

Actually, Morley's distinction between speculation and practice was by no means a new one, having been drawn implicitly by Boethius, and explicitly since the tenth century. But it had previously enjoyed the not uncommon privilege of having been

drawn only that it might be obliterated. Boethius himself did not
distinguish, as did later writers, between *musica activa* and *musica
speculativa*. He did insist, however, that a true musician must
be a man who "on reflection has taken to himself the science of
singing, not by the servitude of work, but by the rule of contemplation." [2] The fifteenth-century theorist Tinctoris insisted
that *"Musicorum et cantorum magna est differentia,"* [3] the musician being the one who had mastered theory as well as practice. Classic sources, too, transmitted the importance of the distinction in both direct and metaphorical ways. Even more strong,
perhaps, than Plato's stress on the importance of speculative
music in education, was the embodiment of a distinction between
reason and blind irrational action in the classic differentiation
of role of the Greek *aulos,* or oboe, and *kithara,* or lyre. *Auloi*
were conventionally Dionysiac, hard to play, provoking to Greek
theorists because of the tuning problems they created, distaste-
ful to the Goddess who disliked the way in which they distorted
the face of the player, and, most important of all, impossible
for the player to sing to. The Apollonian *kithara,* on the other
hand, employed strings (the basis of Greek empirical tuning),
and permitted the player to rationalize his music by identifying
its significance in the words of a sung text. It is perhaps with
this distinction in mind that Bacon turns the story of Orpheus and
the Maenads who destroyed him into a parable of rational science
and blind destructive passion.

For centuries, then, to be described as a musician entailed

[2] Boethius, *De Institutione Musica,* I, 33, tr. O. Strunk, in Oliver Strunk,
Source Readings in Music History (New York, 1950), p. 86.

[3] Joannes Tinctoris, *Diffinitorium Musices* (ca. 1475), in E. de Cousse-
maker, *Oeuvres Théoriques de Jean Tinctoris* (Lille, 1875), p. 489.

being a scholar. To practice the art without understanding the ways in which people were affected by musical sounds was considered irresponsible. Now the authority of Boethius on many general musical questions remained unshaken up through the Renaissance, and his famous tripartite division between *musica mundana, musica humana,* and *musica instrumentalis* helped to blur many distinctions between speculative and practical music in later writers. By *musica mundana* Boethius meant the harmony of the universe, including the cosmological order of elements, astral bodies, and seasons. By human music he meant "that which unites the incorporeal activity of the reason with the body . . . a certain mutual adaptation and as it were a tempering of high and low sounds into a single consonance." [4] This paralleled the cosmic music in causing "the blending of the body's elements." The third category is simply practical music. The first two designate what is in fact not music at all, but figurative ascriptions of a regularity to nature. The harmony of the universe and the tempering of warring elements in the human character are both metaphors from Greek thought, in which the extended sense of the term "harmony" did not preserve the same implications that it holds for us. By and large, we must understand the word *harmonia* as ordered melody, and, when extended, as the rationalized proportions of whole numbers that were seen to generate the intervals between musical tones. Modern usage has reserved for the word "harmony" the sense of the unity that comes from the simultaneous sounding of different tones, and it is probable that it suggested this meaning (although "consonance" was the term then employed) from the tenth century on. But it is *pro-*

[4] Boethius, *De Institutione,* I, 2, in Strunk, *Source Readings,* p. 85.

portion that remains the dominant notion in the Pythagorean view of universal harmony. It was only with the growth of polyphonic music that the idea of harmony as the essence of universal order came to be conceived in terms of the more familiar notion of *e pluribus unum.*

But the application of the term "harmony" remained invariant with respect to the sweeping changes in musical practice that resulted in its utterly different connotations. For example, St. Augustine's *De Musica,* a treatise on prosody, defines music as *"ars bene modulandi,"* the "proper patterning of sound." Using terms such as "concord" and "discord" to refer not to tonal intervals, but to patterns of length in metrical feet, the author classifies all meters with respect to the number of short syllables in *arsis* and *thesis,* respectively. For each type of foot, numerical proportions of *arsis*-"times" to *thesis*-"times" are given and commented upon.[5] It is these proportions involving whole numbers that seem to comprise the universally "musical" character of the prosodic discussions. Over 1,200 years later, Johannes Kepler still clung in a strange way to this element of Pythagoreanism, but with a significant difference. After having pointedly denied the existence of the planetary spheres, and even the circularity of their orbits, Kepler nevertheless sought to demonstrate the "harmony of the universe" by showing how certain ratios involving the angular velocities of the planets (rather than the traditionally used ratios of the diameters of the heavenly spheres) generated musical intervals. He was eager to show that this was not an actual music, but instead, a "harmonious" set of

[5] See W. F. Jackson Knight, *St. Augustine's De Musica: A Synopsis* (London, n.d.), pp. 11–31.

relationships. This was clearly in opposition to the view held by most writers from Aristotle to Montaigne, which regarded the music of the spheres as actual, but unheard, either because it was beyond audible range, or because human ears were dulled to it by custom. But Kepler's concern in justifying his description of the heavenly harmony led him to try to actualize the metaphor in terms of the practical music of his own age. He consequently performed elaborate arithmetical operations on his figures to show how the little melodic fragments he had assigned to each planet could be put into conventional six-part counterpoint, on the grounds that only this could serve as the true test of harmony.[6]

The concept of the music of the spheres was a popular one, passed down from antiquity through Plato, Cicero, and Macrobius' commentary on Cicero's *Somnium Scipionis*. It is of interest not only because of its embodiment of universal harmony, but because of its implications of both human and actual music, Boethius' second and third categories, as well. Historically, Plato's fiction of a singing siren seated on each sphere underwent considerable refinement. In its most widely received form, the doctrine held that the music of the spheres was produced by the rubbing of the supposedly hard, glassy celestial spheres against the ether, their varying sizes and velocities producing respectively varying pitches. The following passage from Cicero might be called the *locus classicus* of the idea of the celestial music:

"What is this loud and agreeable sound that fills my ears?"

"That is produced," he replied, "by the onward rush and motion of the spheres themselves; the intervals between them,

[6] Joannes Kepler, *Harmonices Mundi* (Linz, 1619), V, 6–8.

though unequal, being exactly arranged in a fixed proportion, by an agreeable blending of high and low tones various harmonies are produced; for such mighty motions cannot be carried on so swiftly in silence; and Nature has provided that one extreme shall produce low tones while the other gives forth high. Therefore this uppermost sphere of heaven, which bears the stars, as it revolves more rapidly, produces a high, shrill tone, whereas the lowest revolving sphere, that of the moon, gives forth the lowest tone; for the earthly sphere, the ninth, remains ever motionless and stationary in its position in the centre of the universe. But the other eight spheres, two of which move with the same velocity, produce seven different sounds—a number which is the key of almost everything. Learned men, by imitating this harmony on stringed instruments and in song, have gained for themselves a return to this region . . ." [7]

In commenting on this last sentence, Macrobius remarks that:

Every soul in this world is allured by musical sounds so that not only those who are more refined in their habits, but all the barbarous peoples as well, have adopted songs by which they are inflamed with courage or wooed to pleasure; for the soul carries with it into the body a memory of the music which it knew in the sky, and is so captivated by its charm that there is no breast so cruel or savage as not to be gripped by the spell of such an appeal.[8]

[7] Cicero, *De Re Publica,* VI, 8, tr. C. W. Keyes (Loeb Edition), pp. 271–73.

[8] Macrobius, *Commentary on the Dream of Scipio,* tr. W. H. Stahl (New York, 1952), p. 195.

Thus microcosmic man, imitating in his *musica instrumentalis* or practical music the ideal order of the *harmonia mundi,* can regain in some small way the *musica humana,* the ordering of his being, that characterizes the music of the spheres.

But *musica humana* had another dimension as well. The ethical implications of music, stressed so heavily by Plato, were based on an elaborately reasoned system of classification of the effects of different kinds of melody on listeners. Particular tonal constellations were held necessarily to affect all men in various ways. Long after the death of the Attic musical practices that associated certain types of melody with the singing of certain types of text on particular occasions, the notion of an *ethos* that accompanied each conventional *harmonia* or scale remained an accepted tradition. The Greek ethical doctrines passed into Renaissance thought, aided by a confusion between the Classic scales and the tones or "modes" of liturgical chant. The study of *ethos,* a huge body of Biblical and Classical lore concerning the curative power of music, and the various myths of Orpheus, Arion, Amphion, and Timotheus were continually invoked as evidence of music's beneficial powers. But up through the end of the sixteenth century, the most complete explanations of the reasons for music's ability to move the passions entailed an account of the *musica mundana,* coupled with a characterization of man as the microcosm. In Zarlino's *Institutione* we find that proportion, the essence of both cosmic order and the intervals of practical music, also governed the passions by adjudicating among the conflicting humors, aided by correspondences between modes, humors, and elements. Other arguments were brought up to reinforce this kind of notion. They ranged from correspondences between the rhythm of the alternating up-beat and down-beat of music to the systole and diastole of the human heartbeat, to the somewhat unruly uses of puns on *chorda* "string" and *cor, cordis* "heart" [9] in attempting to demonstrate the effects of music on the soul through the purely physical principle of sympathetic vibration.

The final link in the chain between *musica mundana* and *musica humana* in Renaissance musical speculation is a political one. Plato in his perfect state treated music as if it were ideology, and carefully legislated its uses. Horace had depicted Orpheus and Amphion as the poet-musicians whose art established and governed states, literally, in the case of the latter, from the ground up. Aside from the purely conventional assimilation of political notions into the universal patterns of order, degree, and harmony, the political nature of ideal music enters sixteenth-century thought in peculiar ways. It has been seen that a stringed instrument tended conventionally to connote reason, but in the *Hieroglyphics* of Horapollo, a possibly Hellenistic work first published in 1505, the lyre turns up as the symbol of a man who "binds together and unites his fellows," with the explanation that "the lyre preserves the unity of its sounds." [10] In Alciati's emblem book, so widely distributed and imitated throughout the sixteenth century, there appears the picture of a lute, labelled *"Fides"* above it and *"Foedera"* below, followed by a Latin poem in praise of the great Duke who will some day unite all of Italy. Here another apparently traditional pun on *fides* "trust" and *fides* "stringed instrument" is invoked, and here too, the adaptation of the con-

[9] The possibilities of this word-play may have been initially suggested by Cassiodorus. See *Variae*, II, 40.

[10] *The Hieroglyphics of Horapollo*, tr. George Boas (New York, 1950), p. III.

temporary lute to the symbolic role of the lyre of Antiquity can be seen. These, along with the harp upon which David eased Saul's melancholy, seem to be completely substitutable for each other in certain iconographic contexts. A final stage of symbolic adaptation might be pointed out in the version of Alciati's emblem in Henry Peacham's *Minerva Britannia,* published in 1612. Here, a cut of a bardic harp, labelled in Latin "The Irish Republic to King James," is followed by a little poem in praise of the English monarch which concludes:

Ne'er was the musick of old *Orpheus,* such,
    As that I make, by meane (Dear Lord) of thee,
From discord drawne, to sweetest unitie.[11]

The order of the heavens, political concord, and the organic unity of individual men, each a "little world, made cunningly," were all thus embraced under the extended metaphor of harmony. It was the singular accomplishment of the sixteenth century, however, to incorporate into its *musica speculativa* so much of its practical music. This had for centuries been generating its own forms and conventions independently of the almost hermetically-sealed body of literary discourse that comprised musical speculation. The whole question of the great interest that the sixteenth century took in tuning and temperament, for example, cannot be accounted for by either the mathematical demands of speculative music, or the immediate necessities of the wide-spread uses of instrumental music. And here lies another problem. The music of instruments was, in itself, as

11 Reproduced in *The Mirour of Maiestie,* ed. H. Green and J. Croston (London, 1870), plate V.

common as singing, although the rationalized doctrines of *musica speculativa* tended to reinforce the notion that there was nothing superior to the voices of men. Plato had disapproved of textless music; Aristotle in *De Anima* had maintained that only sounds produced by a windpipe and infused with soul could be meaningful; and Ficino's synthesis of musical doctrine had laid great stress on the importance of the sung texts in understanding the effects of music on a hearer.[12] We might say that vocal polyphony was the model for all music, even at a time when *a capella* singing was merely one of many different practical styles. But by a strange historical irony, it was an overinsistence of the importance of the text by members of the Florentine *Camerata* toward the end of the sixteenth century that led to their experiments in expressive monody, the repercussions of which helped to shape the dominant vocal and instrumental styles of Baroque music. While the quarrels that helped to bring seventeenth-century musical conventions into being were waged on the grounds of expressive textual representation, however, it was eventually the music of instruments that came to be the model for music in general. At the risk of some oversimplification, it might be said that the Renaissance treated instruments as voices, while the Baroque eventually did just the opposite. "There is not any Musicke of Instruments whatsoever, comparable to that which is made of the voyces of Men," writes William Byrd in 1588. After an intervening century of change, the tables are turned, and John Gay can praise womankind by comparing her charms to the acme of expressive effectiveness: "Like the notes

[12] See D. P. Walker, "Ficino's *Spiritus* and "Music," *Annales Musicologiques* I (1953), pp. 131–50.

of a fiddle, she sweetly, sweetly/ Raises the spirits and charms our ears." (Air XXI)

In sixteenth-century England, then, the word "music" could suggest a wealth of speculation to an informed mind. Both a variety of actual practice, and an even more complex intellectual institution were embraced in a dialectic that unified inherited Medieval traditions, more recently acquired information about Antiquity, and the bare facts of how and what people played and sang. Traditional divisions of music into practical and theoretical, or into Boethius' cosmological, psychological, and instrumental were all retained in one way or another. And any answer to the question "What is music?" would involve a confusion between an abstract institution and a concrete practice that a modern philosopher might deplore, but one that we need only consider as an intricate yet unified series of metaphors.

When seen in the light of the richness of sixteenth-century musical thought, the modern academic question of "Shakespeare and Music" tends to be more blinding than the glittering of its generality would warrant. With the aid of the musicological studies of the past thirty years, we are better able than ever before to reconstruct the actual music performed, and referred to, in Shakespeare's plays. The growth of study in the History of Ideas has given us models for understanding how words and customs that have misleadingly retained their forms to this day reverberated differently in various historical contexts. The forays of sixteenth- and seventeenth-century poets into *musica speculativa,* consequently, can now be understood as more than either the fanciful conceits or the transmission of quaint lore that many

nineteenth-century readers took them to be. But the recent
critical traditions that read all of Shakespeare with the kind
of attention previously devoted to other kinds of poetry has
tended to create a third, queer category of symbolic music.
G. Wilson Knight in particular has employed the images of
tempest and music in his criticism to suggest the universal
themes of disorder and resolving, reconciling order. These con-
cepts stem largely from his invaluable early work on the last
plays, in which, trivially speaking, storm and music do appear
to alternate in profound and general ways. But more recently,
Professor Knight has elevated his rather *symboliste* construction
of the word "music" to the heights proclaimed in Verlaine's
manifesto: *"De la musique avant toute chose."* One result of
this has been, I feel, to credit Shakespeare's imagination with the
creation of what, for hundreds of years, had been fairly widely
received ideas. Worse than this, however, has been the failure
to see exactly to what degree Shakespeare's poetic intelligence
utilized these received ideas about music, both speculative and
practical, analyzing and reinterpreting them in dramatic contexts. Finally, and perhaps worst of all, some of Shakespeare's
amazingly original contributions to *musica speculativa* have been
lost sight of.

Twelfth Night represents, I feel, an excellent case in point.
Probably written late in 1600, its treatment of the theme of music
is considerably more complex than that of the plays preceding
it. By and large, the bulk of the references in all the plays is
to practical music, which is cited, satirized, and praised in various
contexts like any other human activity. Of particular interest to
Shakespeare always was the richness of various technical vocabu-

laries, and much of the wit in all but the later plays consists of puns and twisted tropes on technical terminology, often that of instrumental music. Two well-known passages of *musica speculativa* in the earlier plays, however, deserve some comment.

The first of these is Richard II's great speech in Pomfret castle. After likening his prison to the world and to his own body, the King hears music offstage:

> Music do I hear?
> Ha, ha! Keep time. How sour sweet music is
> When time is broke and no proportion kept!
> So is it in the music of men's lives,
> And here have I the daintiness of ear
> To check time broke in a disordered string,
> But for the concord of my state and time
> Had not an ear to hear my true time broke. (V,v,41–48)

"Proportion" here is used in its immediate sense of time-signature, and "time broke in a disordered string" refers to the music he hears playing. But the "disordered string" is also himself, an emblem of the unruled, unruly state. "The concord of my state and time" invokes the musical connotations of "concord" as well—for centuries the word had reverberated with the old pun on "heart" and "string." What the King is saying is that now, in his broken state, he is sensitive to all the nuances of musical order, but formerly, lulled by the metaphorically musical order of his earlier reign, he had been unable to hear the tentative tempi in his own *musica humana*. In this passage an occurrence of practical music is interpreted in perfectly traditional terms, and human and worldly musics are made to coincide, both in Richard's own rhetoric and in the hierarchical imagery throughout the play. The conventional multiplicity of extensions of the term "music" are employed directly, and Richard, aside from the tireless progression of his thoughts, is talking like something out of an Old Book.

The final irony of Richard's soliloquy:

> This music mads me, let it sound no more,
> For though it have help madmen to their wits,
> In me it seems it will make wise men mad.
> Yet blessings on his heart that gives it me!
> For 'tis a sign of love, and love to Richard
> Is a strange broach in this all-hating world. (V,v,61–66)

is reinforced by the fragmentation of "music" into its various categories. The music is maddening because its human and universal roles have not coincided for the King, whose necessary identity with the proper order of the state has been called into question by the fact of his deposition and imprisonment. Bolingbroke, the discord, the untuner, will himself become the well-tuned regulating instrument of state. And finally, the practical music is sundered from its speculative form in Richard's gratitude for the instrumental sounds themselves, which he takes as the evidence of someone's thoughtful care.

I believe that it is this same conventional use of the emblematic stringed instrument in a political context that is at work during a moment in Brutus' tent in Act IV, scene iii of *Julius Caesar*. The boy Lucius has fallen asleep over his instrument after singing for Brutus, and the latter has taken it away from him lest it drop to the ground and break. After the ominous appearance of

Caesar's ghost, Brutus cries out, and the boy half-awakens, murmuring, "The strings, my lord, are false." Brutus, missing the import of this, comments, "He thinks he still is at his instrument," and shakes Lucius fully awake, inquiring after the phantom. But the meaning, I think, is clear, and the false strings are the discordant conspirators, now jangling and out of tune even among themselves. Brutus, who "in general honest thought/ And common good to all, made one" of the varying faction he led, meets the prophetic truth of the boy's half-dreamed image with a benevolently naturalistic interpretation of it.

The even better known music at Belmont in *The Merchant of Venice* shows a more dramatically sophisticated use of *musica speculativa*. In general, the dramatic structure of the whole play hinges on the relationship between Venice, the commercial city where gold is ventured for more gold, and the symbolically golden Belmont, where all is hazarded for love. Belmont is full of practical music in one of its most common sixteenth-century forms. Music used for signalling, the tuckets, flourishes, and sennets familiar to modern readers through stage directions, were not confined to the uses of dramaturgy; it was a matter of actual practice for distinguished persons to be accompanied by their private trumpeters. It is almost as a signal that the song "Tell me where is fancy bred" is employed. Like a nursery-rhyme riddle, it advises against appearances, and cryptically urges the choice of the lead. In a speech preceding the song, Portia's wit analyses and interprets the ceremonial music she has ordered:

> Let music sound while he doth make his choice,
> Then, if he lose, he makes a swanlike end,

Fading in music. That the comparison
May stand more proper, my eye shall be the stream
And watery deathbed for him. He may win,
And what is music then? Then music is
Even as the flourish when true subjects bow
To a new-crowned monarch. (III,ii,43–50)

Here Portia makes the point that the same music can play many
roles, that the institution emerges from the fact as the result
of an intellectual process. She selects two polar institutions, incidentally: music as signal, which plays little or no part in traditional musical speculation, and the myth of the dying swan, a
stock image in romantic lyrics throughout the century. Portia
reaffirms this later on, when she remarks of the music that
Jessica and Lorenzo hear on the bank, "Nothing is good, I
see, without respect./ Methinks it sounds much sweeter than
by day." Nerissa replies that "Silence bestows that virtue on
it," invoking one of the dominant Belmont themes of the de-
ception of ornament, of the paleness more moving than elo-
quence. It is the same theme that prefaces Lorenzo's initiation
of Jessica into the silent *harmonia mundi:*

                Soft stillness and the night
Become the touches of sweet harmony.
Sit, Jessica. Look how the floor of heaven
Is thick inlaid with patines of bright gold.
There's not the smallest orb which thou behold'st
But in his motion like an angel sings,
Still quiring to the young-eyes cherubins.
Such harmony is in immortal souls,

But whilst this muddy vesture of decay
Doth grossly close it in, we cannot hear it. (V,i,56–65)

This is the vision of Plato's Er and Cicero's Scipio. It is significant that the one instance of Shakespeare's troping of the
doctrine is Lorenzo's explanation of the inaudible character of
the heavenly music. Neither of the traditional reasons (acclimatiza-
tion, or the physical thresholds of perception) is given. Instead,
the unheard music is related to immortality, and by extension,
to a prelapsarian condition, a world which, like heaven, need
not conceal its ultimate gold, which even Belmont must do. This
approaches Milton's treatment of the subject in *At a Solemn
Musick*.

Then enter the musicians, to play at Lorenzo's bidding. "I
am never merry when I hear sweet music," says Jessica. She
may, of course, be referring to the concentration demanded by
the soft, "indoor" music of Portia's house musicians, as opposed
to the more strident character of "outdoor" instruments. Lorenzo,
at any rate, answers this with an instructive, though standard,
disquisition on music and the affections, ending on a note of
musica humana with all of its ethical and political connotations:

The reason is, your spirits are attentive.
For do but note a wild and wanton herd,
Or race of youthful and unhandled colts,
Fetching mad bounds, bellowing, and neighing loud,
Which is the hot condition of their blood.
If they but hear perchance a trumpet sound,
Or any air of music touch their ears,
You shall perceive them make a mutual stand,

Their savage eyes turned to a modest gaze
By the sweet power of music. Therefore the poet
Did feign that Orpheus drew trees, stones, and floods,
Since naught so stockish, hard, and full of rage
But music for the time doth change his nature.
The man that hath no music in himself
Nor is not moved with concord of sweet sounds,
Is fit for treasons, stratagems, and spoils.
The motions of his spirit are dull as night
And his affections dark as Erebus.
Let no such man be trusted. Mark the music. (V,i,70–88)

Innuendoes of *musica mundana,* golden, silent, and inaccessible, are intimated at Belmont, where actual music is heard, and where the Venetian incompatibilities of gold and love are finally reconciled, almost as much in the golden music as in the golden ring.

In *Twelfth Night,* however, the role of music is so obviously fundamental to the spirit of the play that it is momentarily surprising to find so little speculative music brought up for discussion. But I think that, on consideration of the nature of the play itself, the place of both active and intellectual music, and the relations between them, emerge as something far more complex than Shakespeare had hitherto cause to employ. *Twelfth Night* is, in very serious ways, a play about parties and what they do to people. Full of games, revels, tricks, and disguises, it is an Epiphany play, a ritualized Twelfth Night festivity in itself, but it is much more than this: the play gives us an analysis, as well as a representation, of feasting. It develops an ethic of indulgence based on the notion that the personality of any individual is a function not of the static proportions of the humors within him, but of the dynamic appetites that may more purposefully, as well as more pragmatically, be said to govern his behavior. Superficially close to the comedy of humors in the characterological extremes of its *dramatis personae,* the play nevertheless seems almost intent on destroying the whole theory of comedy and of morality entailed by the comedy of humors.

The nature of a revel is disclosed in the first scene. The materials are to be music, food and drink, and love. The basic action of both festivity in general, and of the play itself, is declared to be that of so surfeiting the appetite that it will sicken and die, leaving fulfilled the tempered, harmonious self. The movement of the whole play is that of a party, from appetite, through the direction of that appetite outward toward something, to satiation, and eventually to the condition when, as the Duke hopes for Olivia, "liver, brain and heart/ These sovereign thrones, are all supplied, and filled/ Her sweet perfections with one self king." The "one self king" is the final harmonious state to be achieved by each reveller, but it is also, in both the Duke's and Olivia's case, Cesario, who kills "the flock of all affections else" that live in them, and who is shown forth in a literal epiphany in the last act.

The Duke's opening speech describes both the action of feasting, and his own abundant, ursine, romantic temperament. But it also contains within it an emblematic representation of the action of surfeiting:

If music be the food of love, play on.
Give me excess of it, that, surfeiting,

The appetite may sicken, and so die.
That strain again! It had a dying fall.
Oh, it came o'er my ear like the sweet sound
That breathes upon a bank of violets,
Stealing and giving odor! Enough, no more.
'Tis not so sweet now as it was before. (I,i,1–8)

The one personage in the play who remains in a melancholy humor is the one person who is outside the revels and cannot be affected by them. Olivia's rebuke cuts to the heart of his nature: "Thou art sick of self love, Malvolio, and taste with a distempered appetite." Suffering from a kind of moral indigestion, Malvolio's true character is revealed in his involuted, Puritanic sensibility that allows of no appetites directed outward. His rhetoric is full of the Devil; it is full of humors and elements as well. No other character tends to mention these save in jest, for it is only Malvolio who believes in them. Yet real, exterior fluids of all kinds, wine, tears, sea-water, urine, and finally the rain of inevitability bathe the whole world of Illyria, in constant reference throughout the play.

The general concern of *Twelfth Night,* then, is *musica humana,* the Boethian application of abstract order and proportion to human behavior. The literalization of the universal harmony that is accomplished in comedy of humors, however, is unequivocally rejected. "Does not our life consist of the four elements?" catechizes Sir Toby. "Faith, so they say," replies Sir Andrew, "but I think it rather consists of eating and drinking." "Thou'rt a scholar," acknowledges Sir Toby. "Let us therefore eat and drink." "Who you are and what you would are out of my welkin—I might say 'element,' but the word is overworn," says Feste, who, taking offense at Malvolio's characterization of him as a "dry fool" touches off the whole proceedings against the unfortunate steward. The plot to ridicule Malvolio is more than the frolicsome revenge of an "allowed fool"; it serves both to put down the "party-pooper" and to affirm the psychology of appetite and fulfillment that governs the play. To the degree that the *musica humana* of *Twelfth Night* involves the substitution of an alternative view to the fairly standard sixteenth-century descriptions of the order of the passions, an application of the musical metaphor would be trivial, and perhaps misleading. But the operation of practical music in the plot, the amazingly naturalistic treatment of its various forms, and the conclusions implied as to the nature and effects of music in both the context of celebration and in the world at large, all result in some musical speculation that remains one of the play's unnoticed accomplishments.

The actual music in *Twelfth Night* starts and finishes the play, occurring throughout on different occasions and in different styles. The presumably instrumental piece in which the Duke wallows at the opening dampens his desire for it very quickly, but that desire returns before long. Orsino's appetite at the start of the play is purportedly for Olivia, who hungers for, and indulges herself in, her own grief. The Duke's actual love, too, is for his own act of longing, and for his own exclamations of sentiment. Both of these desires are directed outward before the play is over. But until a peculiar musical mechanism, which will be mentioned later on, as has been set to work, the Duke will hunt his own heart, and his desires, "like fell and cruel hounds," will continue to pursue him. The music in Act II, scene iv, is of just such a nature to appease the Duke's extreme sentimentality. Orsino makes it plain what sort of song he wants to hear:

> Now, good Cesario, but that piece of song,
> That old and antique song we heard last night.
> Methought it did relieve my passion much,
> More than light airs and recollected terms
> Of these most brisk and giddy-pacèd times. (II,iv,2–6)

This is a familiar sentimental attitude, the desire for the Good Old Song that nudges the memory, the modern request made of the cocktail pianist, the half-ironic translation in Bert Brecht's *Happy End,* where a singer tries to recapture better days by imploring *"Joe, mach die Musik von damals nach."* Orsino's favorite song, he says,

> is old and plain.
> The spinsters and the knitters in the sun
> And the free maids that weave their thread with bones
> Do use to chant it. It is silly sooth,
> And dallies with the innocence of love,
> Like the old age. (II,iv,44–49)

Actually, the song that Feste sings him is a highly extravagant, almost parodic version of the theme of death from unrequited love. Its rather stilted diction and uneasy prosody are no doubt intended to suggest a song from an old miscellany. "Come away" is a banal beginning, appearing at the start of four song texts in Canon Fellowes' collection. We may also presume that the setting employed was rather more archaic than that of the well-polished lute accompaniments of the turn of the century.

It is just one of these "light airs and recollected terms," however, with which Sir Toby and Feste plague Malvolio in their big scene of carousal (II,iii). A setting of "Farewell, dear heart" appears in Robert Jones' first book of airs, published in 1600. Of the other songs in the same scene, one is a round, a more trivial form of song, certainly with respect to its text, than the sophisticated and intricate lewdness of the post-Restoration catch. The other is a "love song" sung by Feste, and preferred by Sir Toby and Sir Andrew to "a song of good life," perhaps with a pious text. It is of the finest type of Shakesperian song that catches up the spirit of overall themes and individual characters, ironically and prophetically pointing to the end of a plot or bit of action. All of "Oh mistress mine" is in one sense an invocation to Olivia to put off her self-indulgent grief, her courting of her dead brother's memory. In particular, the first stanza refers to Viola, the boy-girl true love, "that can sing both high and low."

Feste's songs to Malvolio in his madman's prison are both of an archaic cast. The first is a snatch of a song of Wyatt's, "A robyn, joly robyn" that was set to music by William Cornish during the reign of Henry VIII. The other one, a parting jibe at Malvolio's cant about the Devil, suggests the doggerel of an old Morality, invoking Malvolio as the Devil himself, and continuing the game of mocking him by appealing to his own rhetoric.

All of these occurrences of practical music function in the plot as well as with respect to the general theme of feasting and revels. The one reference to *musica speculativa* is a very interesting one, however, and leads to the most important aspect of the operation of music in *Twelfth Night*. Olivia is exhorting Viola to refrain from mentioning the Duke to her, and implying that she would rather be courted by his messenger:

> I bade you never speak of him again.
> But would you undertake another suit,
> I had rather hear you to solicit that
> Than music from the spheres. (III,i,118–21)

The citation of the music of the spheres here has the tone of most such references during the later seventeenth century in England. With the exception of poets like Milton and Marvell, who used metaphors from the old cosmology for intricate poetic purposes of their own, the music of the spheres became, in Cavalier and Augustan poetry, a formal compliment, empty of even the metaphorical import that the world view of the centuries preceding had given to it. Just as the word "heavenly," used in exclamations of praise, long ago became completely divorced from its substantive root, the music of the spheres gradually came to designate the acme of effective charm in a performer. It was often employed in compliments to ladies, for example, whose skill at singing made the spheres sound dissonant, abashed the singing angels, and so forth.

As in the case of Dryden's music that would "untune the sky," references to the heavenly harmony had nothing to do with received ideas of music's importance during the later seventeenth century, which were more and more becoming confined to a rhetorical ability to elicit passion, on the one hand, and to provide ornament to the cognitive import of a text, on the other. Purcell likens music and poetry to beauty and wit, respectively; the former can unite to produce the same wondrous effects in song that the latter can in a human being, although the virtues of each are independent. The differences between music and poetry also tended to cluster about the celebrated rift between thought and feeling. Most important of all, traditional *musica speculativa* gradually ceased being a model of universal order, and was replaced by a notion of music as a model of rhetoric, whose importance lay in its ability to move the passions, rather than in its older role of the microcosmic copy of universal harmony. The Apollonian lute-harp-lyre constellation, once an emblem of reason and order, became an instrument of passion in the hands of Caravaggio's leering boys, and in the hands of Crashaw's musician who slew the nightingale by musically ravishing her, as even her avatar Philomela was never so ravished, to death.

With these considerations in mind, the crucial role of Viola as an instrument of such a rhetorical music becomes quite clear. It is unfortunate that we have no precise indication of an earlier version of the play, presumably rewritten when the superior singer Robert Armin entered Shakespeare's company, in which some of the songs may have been assigned to Viola. She declares herself at the outset:

> I'll serve this Duke.
> Thou shalt present me as a eunuch to him.
> It may be worth thy pains, for I can sing,
> And speak to him in many sorts of music,
> That will allow me very worth his service. (I,ii,55–59)

She will be the Duke's instrument, although she turns out to
be an instrument that turns in his hand, charming both Olivia
and himself in unexpected fashion. Orsino is given an excess
of music in Viola. As Cesario, she wins Olivia for her alter
ego Sebastian who is himself, in his few scenes, rhetorically
effective almost to the point of preciosity, and who is likened
to the musician Arion who charmed his way to safety. Viola
is the affective, instrumental, prematurely Baroque music in
Twelfth Night, and it is she whose charm kills off the gour-
mandizing sentimentality in both Orsino and Olivia, directing
their appetites of love outward, in fact, towards herself. Among
the characters to whom Malvolio refers as "the lighter people,"
it is Feste, the singer and prankster, whose pipe and tabor serve
as a travesty of Viola's vocal chords. The operation of Viola's
"music" involves charming by the use of appearances; the
effects of the trickery instigated by Feste are to make Malvolio
appear, until he is undeceived, to be Olivia's ridiculously amorous
swain. (It is, of course, the phrase "To be Count Malvolio" that
appears on his lips after reading the forged letter.) Through
the mechanism of fooling, the travesty of music below stairs,
Sir Andrew is chastened, Sir Toby is soberly married to Maria,
Malvolio is made to act out the madness of which he falsely
accused Feste, and "the whirligig of time brings in his revenges."

The music that brings about the conclusion of the revels is
thus a figurative music. It pervades the symbolic enactment of
indulgence and surfeit in the plot as the actual music, relegated
to its several uses and forms with considerable eye to details of
practice in Shakespeare's own day, pervades the spectacle of
Twelfth Night. The play is about revelry, and, in itself, a revels;

so too, there is music in it, and a working out of a theme in speculative music that strangely coincides with later views on the subject. The *Ursprung* of Viola's music is certainly in the action of the play; it is not to be implied that *Twelfth Night* is anything of a formal treatise, and the music in Illyria all serves its immediately dramatic purposes. Within the context of the play's anti-Puritan, anti-Jonsonian treatment of moral physiology, the role of music seems to have become inexorably defined for Shakespeare. Set in a framework of what, at this point, might be almost coy to call a study in *musica humana,* practical music becomes justified in itself. Free of even the scraps of traditional musical ideology that had been put to use in the plays preceding it, *Twelfth Night* represents a high point in one phase of Shakespeare's musical dramaturgy. It is not until *Antony and Cleopatra* and the last romances that the use of an almost supernatural music, perhaps imported to some degree from the musical *données* of the masque, comes to be associated with the late, great themes of reconciliation and transformation.

PART TWO

The Sound of Poetry

Structure, Sound, and Meaning

EVEN IN THE CONTEXT of these essays, the bare combination of the words "structure," "sound," and "meaning" in a title predicts very little of what a writer is likely to say, or indeed what he is to say it about. This is in part because of an indeterminacy in the current conception of literary structure of sound and meaning—an indeterminacy which it will be one purpose of this essay somewhat to reduce—but in larger part it is because there has been so much recent study and talk about these things by people whose interest in them is not a literary interest, that one cannot be sure what kind of relevance to literary study the result of such a combination will have.

This inconvenience has its advantages. It is well that we should be forced to remember that there is more sound and meaning and structure in the world than the forms and sounds and meanings of literature. Literary studies in the past have often suffered from insufficient recognition of the fact that all these things as they appear in literature are the literary species of phenomena more general in their occurrence, and that from their alternative specifications in other parts of our experience

much may be learned about the characters they manifest when
they appear in literature.

There is hardly a scientist of any kind today who has not
something to tell us about the components of my title—especially
of course about structure—from the biologist and the chemist and
the physicist at one end of the spectrum to the anthropologist,
the sociologist, and the social and the individual psychologist
at what is perhaps the other. The logician, the aesthetician, and
the linguist are the ones who have most to tell us, as they are
also the ones who from their different positions at our sides look
most sharply in our direction while they do. And in fact we
merit some reproach from these enthusiastic and industrious
confreres; from the modern linguist doubtless most of all,
since the advances by which he has in so short a time transformed
his discipline from an almost prescientific humanism to a technical model for a science of its kind are easily accessible to us
and in great part readily convertible to our use.

We should indeed profit more than we have done from all
the various modern increase of knowledge, and of procedures
for advancing knowledge, about the generic realities of which
we study a particular species. But the responsibility for the species
which is the object of our study remains with us. We cannot
be satisfied, and the society we serve will not be adequately
served, by an account of the literary phenomenon which leaves
its description generic or evades the specification of its own
particularity by referring vaguely to more exact descriptions
of merely analogous classes of things. However much we avail
ourselves of the insights and the techniques of the other sciences, we cannot depend upon any of those other sciences to

do our work for us; there will always be work on our materials which nobody can do but ourselves, work which must remain undone if we do not do it. The provision of an adequate description of literary phenomena as such cannot be left even to the neighboring sciences which are closest to us, like aesthetics or the linguistics which I have commended for a potentially most practical utility in assisting our enterprise.

For of course what makes the literary phenomenon the species it is within each of the genera to which it belongs is precisely its overlapping in each of them with other genera to which it belongs equally, so that a descriptive placing of the sub-class cannot be made in terms of any one of the larger classes alone, but must refer it to its place in all such classes as it may be referred to. But the only person who will be concerned with precisely this combination of larger classes, or indeed capable of apprehending it, will be one who is first and more deeply concerned with the smaller class in which the combination occurs and which for scientific identification is constituted by the occurrence of that combination. Such a man will be no scientist if he cannot distinguish, as aspects in the object of his attention, the larger generic class-characteristics; but if he does nothing but this, and so resolves his datum into an abstract enumeration of such characteristics without ever, so to speak, summing them up in a whole number, such science as he arrives at will itself be merely a conflation of partial abstractions, fractional and centrifugal, and not the knowledge of any thing at all.

The literary structure is a linguistic structure. But to the linguist it may look odd, so odd at times that the less intelligent linguists have constructed arguments to establish that it is really not linguistic structure at all. And the literary structure is or may be an aesthetic structure, but to the aesthetician often so problematical that the less intelligent aestheticians in their turn concur with the uninstructed layman in a reluctance to acknowledge it as a "pure" example of aesthetic structure. For such aestheticians the forms of literature present difficulties because the materials of their structure are linguistic materials; for such linguists the problem is that the familiar linguistic materials are in this structure informed by some principle other than that of simply linguistic structure.

Remoter examples of the same behavior are equally instructive. Literary structure, and indeed all linguistic structure, is ultimately a biological phenomenon, for the dynamisms of literature are those of human physical life first of all. In some phenomena of speech-rhythm we may feel very palpably a reflection or incorporation of larger dynamic or organic process; we recognize, for example, in the English shift of accent from one syllable to another, as in "impóssible" and "impossibílity," something analogous to the adjustment we make to keep from falling when we have stumbled. Such things in the speech-construct do in fact interest the biologist, and the physicist. But they do not need these specimens to construct or test their generalizations about them.

I have perhaps too much labored this matter, but it is important. In the complex structure of any work of literature there are many aspects, each of which makes its claim for a specific orientation of interest; or, one might say, the complexity of this structure is that of a complex of structures, each capable of focusing the attention of a different kind of analysis. Some of these differently oriented analyses cover more, some less, of what seems to us to be the total reality of the object with which we are engaged when we have literary experience; some, though partial, seem to be focused sharply upon an aspect of the object that is central to its whole character as we apprehend it; while others seem as plainly to be occupied with something peripheral, and to produce at best curious observations which have little to do with what is distinctive in our experience of literature.

The structure of any thing is simply the totality of all the relations that obtain among the elements of which it is composed. The elements of which literary structures are composed are of course the linguistic elements of sound and meaning. Of the relations that exist or may be established among the various aspects of these elements, those which literary studies have traditionally explored, and those whose exploration continues to offer most promise for literary analysis, can be roughly distinguished more or less in the terms of the tradition as grammatical (i.e., simply linguistic), logical, rhetorical, and poetical (or aesthetic). There are relations, and so also there is structure, of all these kinds in every speech, and of every speech a grammatical analysis, a logical analysis, a rhetorical analysis, and an aesthetic or poetical analysis is possible, whether all of these are equally rewarding as revealing something important in the character of the speech or not.

Every speech is somehow grammatical, since to be speech at all it must conform to the grammar, in a broad sense, of some language; in the terms of De Saussure, every *parole* must conform to the norms of a *langue*. To its "grammatical" structure a speech owes its "meaning"; it is upon this structure that we base our "interpretation" of the signs that constitute it, finally of the sign that it constitutes. And since it has a meaning, any speech is in some sense, if only negatively, "logical," for to be logical is radically to have meanings in conjunction; ultimately it is to have them in such conjunction that there is a relation among them of what we may broadly call implication. Where such relation is lacking among meanings we say indeed that the meaning is not logical meaning; but to determine this requires logical analysis. Every speech is also somehow rhetorical, since it makes an address to someone (even if it is a soliloquy) or to some thing, and this with a view to some, however minimal, effect; and this is the *discrimen* of the rhetorical. The *discrimen* of the aesthetic, in language the poetical, is coherence of structure simply as such—in the receptor a concern with such coherence—and this too is plainly present in some degree in all speech, partly because there is some kind of coherence in the grammatical and logical and rhetorical structures which are there, partly because quite apart from these structures and, so to speak, across them there are relations among the intrinsic properties of their elements of sound and meaning which together constitute another more or less cohesive structure.

Each of these four categories of relations, as each presents its own particular value, is capable of furnishing a principle of organization to order the speech as a whole. We use rather loose terms to designate the resulting types or classes of speech, but in general where the grammatical principle is primary we say we have common prose or ordinary conversational or practical speech; where the logical principle dominates we call the speech logical exposition or scientific prose; where the dominant principle is rhetorical we speak of propaganda or of artistic or literary prose, as the case may require. In the extreme case of dominance of the aesthetic principle we call the speech a poem, but by normal present usage only in the extreme case. Where the aesthetic principle is so prominent as to overshadow the others, but not operative to the extent of raising the elements of sound to a status roughly coordinate with those of meaning, as in much narrative and drama, we resort to terms which attempt to evade a placing of the speech in the continuum which runs from absolute prose to pure poetry.

This continuum in any case stops short of absoluteness at both ends. There is no speech that lacks aesthetic structuring entirely, and none in which the aesthetic structure has wholly absorbed and consumed the contending alternative structural principles, which always persist in embellishing, or embarrassing, its primary design with more or less irrelevant constructions of their own.

Nevertheless, the power of the aesthetic structure to absorb, if not to consume, is very great. That is why it is impossible to specify the aesthetic principle beyond mere cohesion of structure—which is to say, beyond the mere idea of structure as such, since structure implies cohesion. All the other concerns with language somehow involve concern with structure in language, but in those others this structure has an instrumental function, and serves as a means to something beyond itself. Only the aesthetic interest is a pure concern for structure simply for itself. But structure of any kind whatsoever is therefore a potential object of aesthetic interest; and so rhetorical structure, grammatical structure, even logical structure will serve the aesthetic interest if they are what it finds at hand. But if the

aesthetic principle takes command of them, they are likely
to be transformed; for it is the structure they present, not the
grammar or rhetoric or logic, that is an object of aesthetic interest;
and since none of them is ever pure either, and in each of their
structures there are aspects and relations *they* have not absorbed,
and these of course offer their own intrinsic possibilities for
construction, the impartial appetite of the aesthetic interest will
attempt to realize these possibilities, at the least removing the
checks which inhibited their proliferation under the dominance
of the other principles.

But, though by some hypotheses it may have operated powerfully at the origin of language, the aesthetic principle in language
as we know it sets to work only after the others have left their
mark not only on the linguistic system and its internal relations
but on the very elements themselves, the sounds and the meanings. In speech-constructs generated by non-poetic uses of language, the organizing principle by which these elements are
related together into the cohesion of the construct is a principle
derived not from the nature of the sounds or the meanings themselves—though some provision is always made to avoid doing
violence to these natures—but a principle derived from their potential relation to some act or effect which is achieved or promoted by
their construction thus together, and might at least conceivably
be achieved by a similar use of quite other materials. The acts
and effects which are thus achieved are of course ultimately
social, and the non-poetic speech-construct is an instrument of
social action or interaction. It is social interaction, and the need
of developing a general instrument for it, that produces language itself initially. We may therefore say—and with the modern

linguist's invaluable distinction between the phone and the phoneme in mind we *must* say—that the very sounds of a language, along with its meanings and the system into which it erects them, are the products of social action. The achievement of meaning by the use of given combinations of sound is, moreover, a social effect; it is of course pre-poetic, indeed as many linguists rather overstrenuously insist it is pre-literary, and we shall find by what is only apparently a paradox that in itself this effect as such is always extra-poetic. But once the sounds, and the conventionalized meanings, and the set combinations of these that constitute the syntax, of a language have been established by social action and with a view to social action, they exist as things in themselves, with potentialities for structure in terms of the characters they have in themselves without renewed reference to their places in the system in which they are established. These potentialities may then be realized without reference to, not indeed their social attachments, but their established social functions. They may be ordered together into structures now not with a view to an ulterior effect or act, but simply for the possession and enjoyment of their construction together as such. But this is no simple matter. For in their instrumental functioning too they were necessarily, and often very coherently, constructed together: our very idea of a structure of these things is derived from the structuring they have taken in their instrumental use. Then too, as this use has generated or at least discriminated them as elements available for our perception, it has conditioned our perception of them and determined a character in them which is heavy with social saturation, so that even to perceive them as elements available for this freer construction is to apprehend them at the same time as potential components of a construct which functions as a social instrument. We may speak, as I have, of dealing with these elements as "things in themselves"; but deep in themselves these things are social, and potentially instrumental, and to deal with them as they are in themselves is to accept them so, for without this character which results from their social genesis and involvement they would not exist as the things they are. When we speak therefore of the intrinsic properties and the corresponding relations of the sounds and meanings of language as the basis for an aesthetic or poetic structure in them, it is to properties and relations established in them by their social character as much as to any others that we are in fact referring. Not all their properties and relations, of course, are socially established, and in the character of these elements there remains a great deal that is not socially determined. But there is in the intrinsic nature of the sounds and the meanings of language a social aspect or element. Aesthetic structure in language is free of the social aim of other uses of language as instrumental to social action; but it is by no means free of social attachment, since that is already a constituent of the very nature of the elements of which the structure is composed.

This is to say among other things that *sociality* in language, in sounds as well as meanings, is itself a quality that aesthetic structure may exploit for potentialities paradoxically neglected in its social use. It is to say too that no sound that is part of the system of a language can be without some meaning, if only of this kind.

But society is a larger thing than the language which it uses as an instrument, and the poet has relations with his social environment which are broader than those determined directly by his use of that instrument as his material. The art which produces poetry is moreover itself a member of a social community, the community of the fine arts. Poetry is always a most influential member of this community, but its action within it is by no means unilateral; in the general community of the arts as they flourish at any given time the poetry of that time takes as much as it gives. And just as the individual *parole* conforms to the conventional norms of the *langue,* and the poet too in his *parole* must respect these purely linguistic conventions, so the individual work of art in all the arts conforms to explicit or implicit norms set by convention for artistic form in the given milieu and time, and thus the *parole* which is a poem achieves itself as a poetic structure not merely by satisfying the norms of a *langue* but as much and perhaps more by its satisfaction of the norms current for aesthetic structure in general in its period and place. So it may happen that we learn more about some aspect of the form or structure of a given poem by relating it to analogous structures in the music or the painting or architecture of its time than we should learn by comparing it with other poems.

In all the structural categories of literature, from the grammatical to the poetic, both sounds and meanings are component elements in the structures considered as wholes; even logic must notice the physical aspect of its terms or signs, if only long enough to exclude them from formal consideration. But, though the other non-poetic forms of linguistic structure do not go so far in this as logic does, the relation in them of sounds to meanings is one of definite subordination of the former to the latter. It is a

paradox increasingly embarrassing to modern linguistics that
though all its most important work has been done primarily
with sounds, yet up to the present time all its discrimination of
sounds and sound-combinations has been made in terms of meaning, of the functioning of the sounds and their combinations for
signification. If this is truly a paradox, it is perhaps less true
that it should embarrass the linguist, who has shown an admirable
scientific courage and honesty in his loyal maintenance of an
effective procedure in spite of much hostile criticism and his
own frequent misgivings. For it may well be that the whole of
the actual structure of all grammar is structure of sound, upon
which meaning simply—or complicatedly—supervenes. It is at
least a quite intelligible view of grammatical structure to take
it as having the achievement of meaning as its goal, with the
devices of sound-discrimination and combination as its means,
rather than to conceive it as itself a structure of meanings already
achieved. In all this region we must remember that everywhere
it is sound that means; in linguistic signification the sign-thing
is a structure of sound that is meaningful. To say that it is a
structure of sound which "has a meaning" is harmless enough,
but it is speaking, as the psychologists now say, "projectively."
You will not, in any case, find a meaning out there in the sign
as an identifiable objective thing or aspect of a thing which you
can disengage from the sound; all that you will find in the object
is more or less stable combination of sound, and from this you
get meaning. It is *you* who "have" the meaning in strict language, not the word.

I have noted this, however, not to discredit the idea of an
objectivity in meaning—in another context I should insist that

the acknowledged intersubjectivity of meaning is a kind of objectivity, and we must remember that the spirit of phonemics is to reduce, or raise, the brute objectivity of linguistic sound also to this intersubjectivity—but rather to emphasize the fact that thus in grammar, and in general in the non-aesthetic use of language, sound is very distinctly subordinated in the service of meaning: it functions simply to achieve meaning, and to be effaced in that achievement.

In the poetic use of language, on the other hand, there need be no such subordination of either of these elements to the other. The aesthetic impulse is to structure as such. For structure it requires elements, components; but it requires no particular kind of element, and it will accept whatever it finds at hand. In language it finds sounds, and it finds meanings too, for the case of poetry is not in this respect like that of simple prose grammar which must first produce the meanings it is to have before it can manipulate them, like a plant manufacturing its own food before it can be nourished. Poetry begins with established lexical meanings, and indeed much more than lexical, as well as conventionalized sounds, and impartially manipulates both in structures not provided for by the original contexts of either. The aesthetic structuring of language is of the whole body of language and all its accessories, at least potentially. It is hard to say whether meanings or sounds more often initiate the poetic process, but there is no theoretical reason to suppose any primacy of either. The great fact is that, once the process is begun, all the elements have *a priori* equality. In the individual poem that results, sound may be conspicuously more elaborately structured, and so more important in the total form, than meaning (as in Hopkins' Leaden-Golden Echo), or meaning more than sound; but one cannot predict beforehand in principle—though of course in practice one can more or less, since most poets in fact attempt more on the side of meaning than on that of sound—which way it will be.

But if this is so, if the aesthetic interest is in these matters so democratically, or anarchically, impartial, there is in this fact a clear implication which is too often overlooked: the structure in view where the aesthetic interest is in control must be of a kind as readily obtainable with sounds as with meanings. Such a structure must be of a kind very different from that of logic (for which sounds are of no use at all as materials), or of rhetoric, and even of grammar, though in this grammar vindicates its ancient association with poetry as having more affinity with it than with its sisters in the trivium. Grammar indeed constructs in a way as poetry does, being necessarily very primitive in its initial provisions and procedures; but it shares with rhetoric and logic an external principle of construction derived from its aim at extrinsic efficacy. For poetic construction as such, there is no such external principle—except, of course, the negative one of avoiding or diminishing the effects usually obtained by the prose construct. In practice, theories of poetry which postulate as its end a semantic or pragmatic effect of this extrinsic kind, if they specify this end at all conformably to the facts of our experience of poetry (e.g., as the achievement of "non-conceptual" or symbolic meaning or the like), in fact do no more than phrase in positive language this negative "requirement," which is actually only the accidental result of prescinding from, rather than specifying in some alternative way, the semantic efficacy of prose. The semantic effect of a poetic structure as such is necessarily a "natural" meaning, not a conventional meaning of the sort exemplified by lexical significations; apart from this, there is no theoretical reason why part at least of the total semantic effect (including of course the direct semantic residue of component lexical, logical, and rhetorical elements and structures) of a poem should not be of exactly the same character as some semantic and pragmatic effects of prose. When this is true, to "read" the poem for these effects alone is to read it as prose; to read it as poetry is to prescind from these effects at least so far as to enjoy primarily the structure with which they are involved, and thus open the way to apprehension of the "natural" meaning of the structure as such. What I refer to as aesthetic interest is, however, an interest in the structure as form for direct contemplation, not an interest in the natural meanings which inevitably such structure must have.

The only principle of aesthetic structure is that of pure internal consistency and coherence; I have already said that this means in practice the notion simply of structure as such. And where no extrinsic control is available, the structure must be of what we may call the intrinsic relations of the intrinsic properties of the component elements.

The intrinsic property of sound is first of all to be sound, to be a presence to the ear or the "mind's ear." The intrinsic property most obvious in a specific sound is that it is that sound; and, almost concurrently obvious, that it is not other sounds. The first relation that appears among sounds, then, is the relation based on qualitative differentiation among sounds, the difference of the phonemes in the language, or the sounds roughly represented in its alphabet, between vowel and consonant, voiced and unvoiced, and the like. Structure based on such differentiation, a pattern of samenesses and differences, of likeness and unlikeness in these qualities of sounds, is the most conspicuous design in such lines—I choose from a foreign language, close to our own, since that will more strikingly exhibit this kind of relation—as "Wie in Glas eingegossene Gärten, klar, unerreichbar," or "Mir wie ein Hund unheimlich stumm und fremd."

Next apparent among intrinsic properties of sound is that of being just so much sound, and, by virtue of that, just so much more or so much less than other sounds, either in a quantitative continuum of all sounds or in a relatively immediate context of particular sounds. The play of relations of this kind, which are the foundation of all rhythmic structure however complex, though audible of course in the lines I have just quoted, is better exhibited in our own language because sense is the primary factor in directing the greater sounds to gather lesser sounds round them to make groups which again have quantitative masses or sizes that vary, and shapes that naturally vary but may be made by art to repeat themselves. This is the chief operation of the quantitative aspects of sound—to create dynamic pressures which force the qualitatively differentiated single sounds to gather into unitary masses and forms, and then in turn together to form larger masses and forms.

The groups that result may be clearly distinct, yet flowing together: "China was tranquil when her rulers understood these few pages . . ." or flowing so together that though we feel their nuclei as centers, and the rise of the mass of each group to the center, we feel no break or clear demarcation between them as they

flow: "Finding the precise word for the inarticulate heart's
tone means not lying to oneself . . ." or "Insistence on birth
at the wrong season is the trick of evil . . ." Their flow may
be broken: "To die, to sleep;/ To sleep: perchance to dream . . ."
or even sharply broken: "Let us not, for God's sake, be vulgar
—we haven't yet, bad as it is, come to *that*. . . ." They may be
partly flowing, partly broken: ". . . he moved to the chimney-
piece, where his eyes, for a little, intently fixed the small ashy
wood fire. When he raised them again it was, on the observation that the beautiful clock on the mantel was wrong, to con-
sult once more his watch, and then give a glance, in the chimney
glass, at the state of his moustache, of which he twisted, for a
moment, with due care, the ends."

Notice how differently too, when as I have said art contrives the
repetition of the shapes in these sound-groups, the sense may
"variously draw out" the sound-mass itself from group to group:
"Dainty fruits, though sweet, will sour/ And rot in ripeness,
left untasted . . ." or "The brotherless Heliades/ Melt in such
amber tears as these."

Certainly unless we see that crests and recessions in the sense
here are in correspondence with those we find in the sound
we are not apprehending the structure of the meaning. The
constant correspondence of emphasis in the sense with stress
in the sound in natural speech indeed suggests a correspondence
between quantity in sound and an aspect in the meaning which
we may also call quantitative. I have said that in the sound it
is this quantitative dynamism which aggregates and fuses the
qualitatively distinct elements together into the forms which
cumulate, by the same dynamism, to the total form of the whole

structure; it is likely that a similar dynamism operates in the
meaning, with nuclei of semantic intensity massing the qualitatively distinct individual elements of meaning into similarly
cumulative structures. It was thus, in fact, that ancient rhetorical
and prosodic analysis conceived the structure of the period with
its wavelike form and the minor cumuli of its cola and commata.

The stresses generated by sense-emphasis may even in a
speech full of logical pressures make a kind of music almost
of the logic itself:

> That a man dies when deprived of air, is not an accident of
> his person, but a law of his nature; that he cannot live with-
> out quinine or opium, or out of the climate of Madeira, is
> his own peculiarity. If all men everywhere usually had the
> yellow fever once in their lives, we should call it (speaking
> according to our knowledge) a law of the human con-
> stitution; if the inhabitants of a particular country com-
> monly had it, we should call it a law of the climate; if a
> healthy man has a fever in a healthy place, in a healthy
> season, we call it an accident, though it be reducible to the
> coincidence of laws, because there is no known law of their
> coincidence.

There is much more here, of course, than a pattern of stresses
in the sound. The qualitative recurrences count for as much as
stress; and of course where repetition of the qualitatively differentiated sounds extends itself, it involves either semantic
repetition also (as in the series *healthy . . . healthy . . . healthy*),
or occasional chiastic tension between the relation of sounds and
the relation of the meanings they present (as in *no known*). The

more obvious chiasmus, *coincidence of laws—law of their coincidence* appears exactly paralleled in the sense and in the qualitative structure of the sounds, subtly varied or distorted but yet generally similar in the quantitative structure of the sound. The resolution of bound elements which such inversion involves, here subtly pointed by the intrusion among the resolved elements of a new unit (*their*) has of course a powerful structural effect, illustrated several times elsewhere in this short passage; in the recombination of such resolved elements likeness and difference may play against each other almost to fusion in a higher identity of opposites.

Structures thus impressive as pure design or pattern occur in the logical prose of actual logicians at their most logical. Hear for a moment Petrus Hispanus, in his *Summulae Logicales* (6, 22): "In via autem naturae humanitas mea per se alia est ab humanitate tua, sicut animalitas mea, per quam humanitas mea est in me, alia est ab animalitate tua, per quam cadit humanitas tua in te . . ."

It is not easy in such passages as these to disengage structure of meaning from structure of sound. One reason for this is doubtless the fact that, though sounds and meanings are absolutely distinct things and can as such never be interrelated, much less fused,[1] yet some at least of the primary intrinsic properties of the two elements are so nearly the same that interrelations among them of these properties alone suffice to constitute a common

---

[1] Onomatopoeia is a coincidence of two *meanings* or strands of meaning, one "natural" or extralexical, the other conventional lexical signification; concord or conformity of this sort between *sound* and meaning is an impossibility. The concord is of natural, or at least prelexical or paralexical, *suggestion* of the sound with its conventional reference.

structure in which both participate. Quantity or intensity in sound has its analogue in intensity in meaning, which may therefore be thought of as quantitative (though we are far at present from the prospect of applying measurement to it); and the relation of emphasis in the sense to stress in the sound is the best corroboration of the hypothesis I have suggested. Perhaps it may be its only corroboration. But I think we shall find much more if we give the kind of attention to literary structure of meaning that linguists of the past generation or two have given to linguistic structure of sound.

The first steps in such a process must of course be to determine exactly what the real units are into which a semantic structure can be resolved, which of these is the constant minimal unit, and what minimal or primary combinations of such units occur as the foundation—and the type?—of the larger structures for description of which our present techniques afford approximations to relatively adequate gross analysis. This is probably as much as I should say of this, for I am not in a position to sketch out summary prolegomena to any future science of meaning in literature. But one or two minimal and gross approximations, propaedeutic let us say to conceivable prolegomena, I cannot resist hazarding.

The essential thing in a structure of meaning is that there be meanings in it, that meanings be initially established. What it is to establish a meaning we hardly know; but it is clear that every meaning once established is itself a structure, whether its structure is simple, as in "direct" or literal meanings, or complex as in a trope. For meaning, being reference, is entirely relational, itself a relation and founded upon relatedness of other things, to which it refers and by means of which it refers. This is to say that recognition of meanings is an exercise in that discrimination, and relating, of likeness and unlikeness which are the basis of all structure, including structure of sound. Professor Quine has made two large classes of the major problems of meaning, one class of those connected with the having of meaning (significance) and one class of those connected with likeness and unlikeness in meaning (synonymy).[2] This is a useful division, and I do not mean to impugn it when I say that these two are in the end one thing, or the obverse and reverse of the same thing, and that we become aware of the two concurrently. To "have meaning" is to have like-or-unlike meaning; to be a given meaning is to be the same or different from other meanings, just as to be a sound is to be a given sound like some other sounds and unlike others. As the play of sounds occurs within a continuum in which each sound has its place as like or different from other sounds, so all the play of meanings occurs in a manifold of semantic likeness and difference. Relation of this kind among meanings is the semantic analogue of qualitative relation among sounds; as, we may say again, relation among meanings in terms simply of the presence or intensity of meaning is the semantic analogue of quantitative phonetic relation.

But as to the qualitative relation, or discrimination, of meanings, the relational or structured nature of meaning as such seems to import an involvement of likeness and unlikeness at a level

[2] W. V. Quine, *From a Logical Point of View* (Harvard, 1953), esp. pp. 11–12 and p. 48. (My identification of *meaning* with *reference* above implies no dissent from Quine's insistence upon discrimination of the two things he calls by these names; I prefer, for the present at least, not to use these terms as he uses them.)

or a stage anterior to that of its impingement in the case of sound. All single meanings are either "direct" or "indirect," either "literal" or "tropical," from the very first moment of their full establishment. But this means that from the very first meanings can be divided into these two classes in terms of the inclusion in the structure which constitutes them of either (in the case of direct or literal meaning) nothing but likeness, or (in the case of tropes) both likeness and unlikeness. Pure structures of unlikeness seem, as we should suppose *a priori,* not to occur: when we say "the opposite" of what we "intend," we produce the trope of irony, which like all tropes involves at least enough of what it is "the opposite of" to assure us of the opposition. In compound structures where more than a single "word" is involved, there is—I suppose again naturally—even less occasion for pure unlikeness; paradox and oxymoron are further from such an extreme than irony. When we conceive all meanings as occupying a place in a continuum stretching from the extreme represented by irony to the other extreme of entire absence of irony or plain "literal" utterance, we must observe that most meanings occur at a fair remove from both extremes. It is the middle range where likeness and unlikeness are more or less balanced, the range of "analogy," that is most crowded. Doubtless it is natural enough that the various patterns of analogy and substitution have most preoccupied students of literature; and doubtless the preoccupation is legitimate, if we judge as we must by the insights into form that the study of metaphor alone, the chief of the tropes of analogy, has produced.

It is an accident that my quotations from Rilke and Von Hoffmansthal both included the word for "like," *wie.* They

are in any case two of the most "poetic" lines I know. So far as
it is true, is something of this kind the meaning of Ezra Pound's
statement that "Great literature is simply language charged with
meaning to the utmost possible degree"? The poet may be thus
plain and say "like . . .": "Like to the lark . . . ," "Like to the
Pontic sea . . . ,"—or, less directly, "That time of year thou mayst
in me behold . . . ," or simply, "Put out the light, and then
put out the light . . ."

Some such differentiation of basic characters or qualities and
of basic quantities or intensities must be the foundation of the
larger structures of meaning as it is of the larger structures of
sound. And in the composition of those larger structures the
same general processes must be involved in the one as in the
other: grouping of the qualitatively distinct elements, by means
of the dynamism of quantitative differences, into units or systems
more or less internally cohesive, and of these together in series
or in larger systems until a whole is achieved in which these
in turn are the beginning, middle, and end. And through all
such composition a single principle must operate, that of the
apparently simple relation of identity and diversity, of sameness
or likeness and difference or unlikeness, providing the forms
of repetition, recurrence, balance, equivalence, congruence, on
the one hand, and on the other those of opposition, contrast,
tension, conflict.

The forms produced by such configuration of these elements
impress us very differently when they are of the magnitude of
Hamlet and when they are the size of a word that Hamlet
speaks. But since *Hamlet* is a construction of words, its construction cannot be radically different from the construction of

a word. I have been implying all along that we may increase our knowledge of the nature of the larger construction by more assiduous study of the smaller, and of course also by converting to use in our study of the larger what we, or others, already know of the smaller. This applies generally to both study of sound and study of meaning. But I think I have throughout implied equally, what I certainly believe, that we can learn a great deal more than we now know about structures of meaning from the study of structures of sound. This generalization too applies broadly to all aspects of the two vast fields, and to non-poetic as well as to poetic uses of language. But it is of course especially applicable in the study of poetry. For, as I have also implied, the semantic structure of poetry is more like the poetic structure of sounds than it is like the semantic structures of logic, or of rhetoric, or even of grammar so far as those exist.

Spenser and Milton: Some Parallels and Contrasts in the Handling of Sound

SPENSER THE MELLIFLUOUS, Milton the "organ voice of England": these two clichés are well-established and, like many clichés, they contain an element of truth. The contrast between the smooth fluency of *The Faerie Queene* and the sonorous power of *Paradise Lost* is, on the whole, a very real one. Both poems belong to the same general tradition of the Renaissance epic. Milton learned much from Spenser, whom he regarded as "a better teacher than Scotus or Aquinas"; in his early poetry he was a Spenserian. Yet as we approach *Paradise Lost,* we should be hard put to it to discover two consecutive lines that could possibly be mistaken for Spenser's work. The use of language in all its complexity accounts for the difference, and scholars have devoted much time, labor, and insight to the study of each manner. What will be attempted at present is an examination of the two styles from one specific point of view, that of sound. Not the treatment of sound even in all its major aspects: sound is an infinitely intricate phenomenon, as all students of it know. I shall touch upon a few points only, starting with some of the simplest. Even so, it may prove possible to unravel a few tangles and make some contributions towards a more exact definition of the ways in which the two poets' individualities are manifested. It may appear that the "honeyed" flow of Spenser's verse contains more contrasts, even grittiness, and sometimes more impetuosity, than is usually assumed. It may perhaps also be demonstrated with somewhat greater technical precision than has so far been done that the "sudden blazes," the strength and majesty of Milton even at their most thunderous and overwhelming, in their phonetic aspect are largely the results of a consistent technique which is the very opposite of impetuous.

Let us begin with the most general features, vowels and consonants. Vowels, with their variations in pitch, length, and overtones, almost literally provide "music," whereas consonants, much more tangible and produced with a more clearly perceptible effort of articulation, supply what may be metaphorically called body, mass, and weight. Accumulated consonants—consonant clusters—create an effect of special massiveness and strength, although there are differences in this respect between voiced and unvoiced consonants, plosives and continuants, liquids and sibilants, to mention only a few of the possible distinctions.

One might expect two poets as different as Milton and Spenser to differ appreciably in the relative amounts of vowels and consonants they use. Surprisingly enough, such an expectation would be utterly wrong, if my examination of extreme consonantal and extreme vowel effects in a series of passages from *The Faerie Queene* and *Paradise Lost* affords any criterion. What

I counted in 1,500 lines of each poem were stressed syllables beginning or ending with consonant clusters, and such syllables
beginning or ending with vowels. I excluded cases in which there
was some doubt as to the syllables to which some of the consonants
belonged. Thus, *revenge, vengeful* were counted, but not *venge-
ance* or *avenger*. The results for both poems were almost precisely identical: 175 instances per hundred lines in *The Faerie
Queene,* and 174 in *Paradise Lost* of syllables with clusters, and
no difference at all—91 cases per hundred lines for both poets
—in the figures for syllables with initial or final vowels. These
coincidences are so striking that one suspects that what they
reflect is the structure of the language itself rather than the
tastes and preferences of the two authors.

This, however, is where the resemblance begins and ends. A
closer scrutiny of the exact positions within the syllables of
massed consonants and of vowels unenclosed in a consonantal
frame reveals two diametrically opposed tendencies. Spenser
loves to place his consonant clusters at the beginning, as in
plain, whereas Milton prefers them at the end, as in *first.*[1] The
vowels in Milton, rather more often than in Spenser, are pre-

---

[1] The passages examined are *The Faerie Queene,* I, i; I, ii; I, iii, st.
1-10; I, xi: *Paradise Lost* I, 1-500; II, 1-500; VI, 1-500. Essential figures
(counting only metrically stressed syllables) are: for initial clusters—
Spenser 1,191, Milton 863; initial clusters at line end—Spenser 389, Milton
277; final clusters—Spenser 1,408, Milton 1,733; final clusters at line end—
Spenser 371, Milton 601; syllables beginning with vowels—Spenser 666,
Milton 859; such syllables at line end—Spenser 57, Milton 74; syllables
ending with vowels—Spenser 694, Milton 501; such syllables at line end—
Spenser 199, Milton 114; total number of clusters—Spenser 2,599, Milton
2,596; total number of stressed syllables beginning or ending with vowels
—Spenser 1,360, Milton 1,360.

ceded only by single consonants or by no consonants at all. In Spenser, on the contrary, the tendency is to avoid anything heavier than a single consonant after the stressed vowel, which, of course, makes the vowel element more conspicuous. The contrast, reduced to its essentials, then, is: in Spenser, a vigorous initial consonantal effect followed by weakened consonantism or none—decrescendo; in Milton, an unobtrusive beginning followed by a strong consonantal finale—crescendo. The Miltonic formula is represented by such words as *earth, arms, Heav'ns, world, rowld, burnt;* that of Spenser by *prey, stray, bray, speed, steed, smoke, stroke.* Certain linguistic habits of Spenser's enhance this characteristic trend, especially his retention of vowels normally omitted in such forms as *framèd, crownèd, middèst,* which prevents the formation of clusters after the stressed vowel. The predilection of the mature Milton for syncopation and elision, on the other hand, enables him to crowd more and more consonants into the end of his syllables: *chos'n, grav'n, count'nance, breath'st, call'st.* Milton's growing dislike of syllabized *-ed* endings—special favorites of Spenser's—makes for similar results. Early lines like "In unreprovèd pleasures free" still have a quasi-Spenserian ring. In *Paradise Lost* such lines are scarce and become scarcer as the poem proceeds. The vowel barriers between the consonants are progressively removed.

I select a few passages in which the divergent patterns are represented somewhat more fully than usual. First some from Spenser:

> Upon a great adventure he was bond,
> That greatest Gloriana to him gave,
> That greatest glorious queene of Faery Lond . . . (I,i,3)

A shadie grove. . . . .
Whose loftie trees, yclad with sommers pride,
Did spred so broad, that heavens light did hide . . . (I,i,7)

He so disseized of his gryping grosse,
The knight his thrillant speare againe assayd
In his bras-plated body to embosse,
And three mens strength unto the stroake he layd;
Wherewith the stiffe beame quaked, as affrayd,
And glauncing from his scaly necke, did glyde
Close under his left wing, then broad displayd. (I,xi,20)

Alliteration or semi-alliteration (as in *trees, pride, spred, broad*) here helps to emphasize the initial clusters. Contrast between unvoiced sounds in the clusters and voiced final consonants or vowels without consonants at the end of the syllable increases the initial emphasis (*trees, spred, speare, three,* etc.). The disburdened vowels that follow the clusters ring out freely. In the last quotation the excessive massing of clusters blunts rather than strengthens their impact. Spenser's effort becomes too obvious. The effect of the topheavy syllables, at least for one reader, is somewhat contrived, yet primitive, even awkward.

Milton's favorite type of syllable is less conspicuous, partly because it is more common in English. It is only in extreme concentrations of it that we become fully aware of its presence, for example, in the much discussed line "Rocks, Caves, Lakes, Fens, Bogs, Dens, and shades of Death." Here all syllables, metrically stressed as well as unstressed, save only the last two, are of this kind. Usually the cumulative effect, though strong, does not advertize itself. What we feel is volume and weight without quite realizing the way this result is achieved:

> He scarce had ceas't when the superiour Fiend
> Was moving toward the shore; his ponderous shield
> Ethereal temper, massy, large and round,
> Behind him cast. . . . (I,283–86)

> High on a Throne of Royal State, which far
> Outshon the wealth of Ormus and of Ind,
> Or where the gorgeous East with richest hand
> Showrs on her Kings Barbaric Pearl & Gold . . . (II,1–4)

>   and the Orbes
> Of his fierce Chariot rowld, as with the sound
> Of torrent Floods, or of a numerous Host. (VI,828–30)

Spenser eagerly displays his technique, whereas that of Milton is far less ostentatious by its very nature. The former's delight in initial consonantal flourishes contrasts markedly with Milton's seemingly unemphatic reliance on gradually increasing consonantal strength.

The two methods are even more sharply contrasted in the line endings of the two poets, where the frequencies of Spenser's prevocalic and Milton's postvocalic clusters are more than doubled. Such an intensification of a dominant tendency does not come as a surprise in Spenser, since the rhymed endings are naturally treated with special care. It is more interesting to find the same trend in Milton's blank verse. It runs counter to the traditional notion that for him the individual line was a very subordinate unit intended to be submerged in the long flow of his paragraphs. Spenser's method, with its emphasis on the beginning of the syllable, may quite possibly be connected with the native alliterative tradition, to which, unlike his master Chaucer, he so patently belongs: a great number of his line endings alliterate with words within the line. In *The Pearl*, for example—a poem which perhaps influenced him—a similar combination of rhyme with even more pronounced alliteration yields closely parallel results. It would be tempting to regard Milton's approach as an outcome of his long apprenticeship in the use of rhyme, where the phonetic point of gravity should tend towards the end of the syllable. Unfortunately for the neatness of the contrast, such a theory seems untenable. His early verse is still fairly close to Spenser's practice: the features noted do not become prominent until after his Italian journey. This seems to support the view advanced by F. T. Prince [2] that he was influenced by the Italian ideal of *asprezza,* masculine strength, one of the main manifestations of which, according to Tasso, is "the sound, or, so to speak, the clamor of the double consonants, which strike the ear in the last syllable of the verse." Tasso's examples make it clear that he means postvocalic clusters. These he considers more than anything else to be conducive to "grandezza, e magnificenza nelle rime toscane."

There is more evidence than Mr. Prince has cited to confirm his theory. Tasso, like Milton, does not like to encumber the endings of his *versi sciolti* too often with prevocalic clusters. Moreover, the great majority of his final accumulations of consonants avoid extreme harshness by being voiced: *langue, rimbomba, mondo, eterno, Padre, interna, armi.* This is equally true of Milton, four-fifths of whose final clusters are voiced: *besides, deceiv'd, Peers, Arms, wilde, round, flames, comes.* In Spenser, about half of the final clusters contain unvoiced consonants, which

[2] *The Italian Element in Milton's Verse* (Oxford, 1954), Chapter 8.

every now and then are crowded at line end for brisk or grotesque effects: *betakes, witch, makes, pitch, unlich, stamp, switch, champ, ramp* (I,v,28); *came, lept, same, stept, kept, flasht, swept, washt, dasht* (II,vi,42). Such deliberate deviations from heroic grandeur savor less of Tasso than of Ariosto: *chioccia, croccia, roccia; cerchio, superchio, coperchio; braccia, slaccia, faccia.* This, we feel—and closer examination confirms our feeling—is the kind of thing that Milton's sense of decorum would very seldom permit him to do. Weight rather than excessive sharpness, gravity rather than harshness, strength combined with sonority characterize his heroic verse.

It seems very likely that Milton's thorough training in Latin versification inclined him to accept the Italian method of achieving phonetic magnificence. The quantitative strengthening of the body of his stressed syllables makes his verse often sound like classical hexameters: it adds to their Virgilian quality, so frequently felt yet so hard to define.

Spenser, as has just been seen in his treatment of consonant clusters, is far from disguising his art. He wants his effects to be duly noticed. This is true of him almost throughout. He likes to accumulate devices of the same kind, to show off his skill in playing with them, and to arrange them as clearly and geometrically as possible, which often leads to symmetry. His harmonious, or, to quote Arnold Stein, his "horizontal" style has often been contrasted with the jerky, uneven, "vertical" manner of other poets, above all Donne. This distinction, though valid, probably needs some qualification. Numerous contrasts, heavily underscored by repetition, are embedded in the stream of Spenser's verse. However, his vividly contrasting effects are distributed rather evenly, with few large-scale culminations. Our mind is not as a rule focused on any one point for any length of time —usually just for a moment or two; but the poet often takes great care to make the pictures and patterns presented as intense as possible while they last. This is seen as clearly in his handling of sound as in other respects.

In the two opening stanzas of the first canto of his poem Spenser portrays the Redcrosse Knight. One stanza describes the youthful dash and bravery of the "full jolly Knight," whereas the following stanza—almost depicting another person—emphatically turns to the more pensive, "too solemne sad" aspects of his character. The phonetic designs of these stanzas are sharply differentiated. Stanza 1 has a superabundance of "clear," high-pitched vowels, [i] and [ī]. Seven rhyme words have them: *shielde, fielde, wield, bitt, yield, sitt, fitt.* Consonance stresses the likeness of the vowels: "*silver shielde*," "Where*in* old *din*ts of *deepe* woundes *did* remaine," "*seem*d . . . *sitt*," "*fierce . . . fitt.*" [3] The second stanza switches over to equally strongly marked low-pitched vowels, [o], [ɔ], [ɔ̄]. Five rhyme words have one of these vowels: *bore, Lord, wore, ador'd, scor'd.* The r's of this series stand out against the l's of the previous one. The contrast, passing from one end of the vowel scale to the other, could hardly be missed by the most casual reader.

Similar dominant motifs in heavy accumulations, which may extend through more than one stanza, form part of Spenser's stock-in-trade. In many instances, the first and last rhymes of a stanza—a total of five endings out of nine—are the same.

[3] It also makes us compare differences in the vowels, even such minute ones as that between [i] and [ī], as in *seemd, sitt.*

Stanza 42 of the opening canto has the endings *spake, vaine, awake, paine, againe, speake, braine, weake, break.* The next stanza has *wake, name, quake, blame, came.* Such large blocks of similar sound structure inevitably single out the passages involved.

Frequently abundant alliteration forcibly welds several lines into distinctive units. For instance:

> That when he heard, in *gr*eat perplexitie,
> His *g*all did *gr*ate for *gr*iefe and high disdaine;
> And knitting all his force, *g*ot one hand free,
> Wherewith he *gr*ypt her *g*orge with so *gr*eat paine. . . .
> (I,i,19)

Here assonance or complete identity of some of the linked syllables remarkably emphasizes the alliterations: *great, grate, great; gall, got, gorge; griefe, grypt.* Note the symmetrical play on the three vowels and the almost completely regular alternation of clusters with single consonants: *great, gall, grate, griefe, got, grypt, gorge, great.* The series begins and ends with the same word. This, it seems, is a craftsman's very deliberate demonstration of his superior skill in organization; yet the passion for copious repetition is there for anyone to see.

This passion often reaches a point at which nearly all conceivable figures of phonetic repetition may be compressed—one would sometimes like to say, squeezed—into seemingly inextricable tangles of similar sounds, which may even impede articulation unless they are read slowly, as Spenser in most cases probably wanted them to be read:

> The willow *worne* of *forlorne* para*mours* (I,i,9)

Furthest from *end then, when* they neerest *weene* (I,i,10)

Most *loth*som, *filth*ie, *foule,* and *full* of *vile* disdaine (I,i,14)

Where *plain none* might her *see,* nor *she see* any *plaine* (I,i,16)

And next her wrin*k*led *sk*in rough *sack-cl*oth wore (I,iii,14)

There is much art in most of these apparent tangles, however. A maximum of consonantal repetition with but vowel variation appears in a device used in the expressive, if not conventionally beautiful line "Most lothsome, filthie, foule, and full of vile disdaine." This verse seems clogged with reiterated consonants, but their arrangement is orderly. Three different vowels are placed in an identical consonantal frame, *f-l.* Gerard Manley Hopkins and Wilfred Owen systematically revived the use of this figure of sound.[4] It is capable of at least two formal functions: it strongly impresses on the mind the consonantal pattern, but it also brings out vividly the differences in the vowels, the only variables in the design in its pure form. Spenser often uses this device with much ingenuity in his line endings, interweaving two or more pairs of this type: *fyre, myre, respire, farre, marre, starre* (II,vi,44); *were, beare, feare, ward, unbar'd, far'd* (IV,ix,15). Correspondences within the lines may further complicate the pattern:

On th' other *side,* in one con*sort,* there *sate*

·   ·   ·   ·   ·   ·   ·   ·   ·   ·

Disloyall Treason, and *hart*-burning *Hate;*

---

[4] See D. I. Masson's interesting paper "Wilfred Owen's Free Phonetic Patterns: Their Style and Function," *Journal of Aesthetics and Art Criticism,* XII (1955), 360–69. Masson calls the type in question "circumsyllabic."

> But gnawing Gealosy, out of their *sight*
> *Sit*ting alone, his *bit*ter lips did *bight* . . . (II,vii,22)

Side, consort, sate, hart, Hate, sight, sitting, bitter, bight—nine close echoes exactly or approximately conforming to the type described: this seems abundance indeed. One wonders, however, whether this is not at least in part gratuitous abundance—a typically Elizabethan display of verbal dexterity, stimulating in its exuberance but not necessarily expressive of anything in particular. Only a few of the important words—*hart, Hate, bitter, bight*—are made to stand out in vivid relief.

By setting off one pattern, one dexterously woven arabesque against another, Spenser in any case achieves variety, and by spacing his varied designs carefully he attains unity of style and total atmosphere. But since he practices little economy to begin with, painting mainly in bright primary colors, so to speak, when he needs special vividness he is forced to heighten his coloring to the utmost. There are limits to this procedure of brightening, since the resources of language are not boundless. Milton, recognizing these limits of his medium, shows himself to be a master of strict economy in exploiting its possibilities to the best advantage. He subdues his phonetic background, thus needing but little intensification to affect us strongly. His intense effects are usually concentrated at the important focal points. With a slight stylistic effort he seems to be able to obtain the most momentous results.

Milton's rhetorical training must have been very like Spenser's, and he had studied the latter's practices with an accomplished expert's eye, so of course he knew all his technical tricks. He used most of them himself. It would be tedious to quote parallels.

The important point is that he employed such devices more sparingly and that in general he toned them down.[5] The individual line in *Paradise Lost* is far less loaded with consonantal repetition than in *The Faerie Queene*. This applies above all to alliteration. Milton manages with not much more than half the amount of stressed alliterations within the same line that Spenser uses, keeping the alliterating syllables farther apart.[6] Identical initial consonant clusters—the most intense form of alliteration —are rare in his line. The repeated consonants more often than in Spenser appear not in the prominent opening syllable of a word but in the middle of longer words ("In*v*oke thy aid to my ad*v*entrous song," "I*ll*umine, what is *l*ow raise and support"). Assonance, more elusive than consonance, occurs almost as often as in Spenser but is less frequently supported by consonantal

[5] In his treatment of Milton's style in *Paradise Lost and the Seventeenth Century Reader* (New York, 1948), B. Rajan points out consonantal accumulations in Milton's poem, quoting Book I, 44–47, where he finds thirteen instances of *m* and *n,* eleven of which, he says, occur in combination with an *i* or an *o.* As it happens, only seven of these instances appear in stressed syllables, the rest being half-concealed in unstressed positions. The vowels vary much more than Mr. Rajan suggests, for the *i* stands for several sounds, and the unstressed *o*'s are unlike the stressed ones. The critic confuses spelling with pronunciation. The technique here is typical of Milton: it is anything but obtrusive, but the cumulative effect is strong.

[6] Alliterations in stressed syllables (within the same line) in the same samples as above: Spenser 1,906 syllables; Milton 1,165 syllables. Assonance: Spenser 3,050 syllables; Milton 2,941 syllables. If linkages of long and short vowels and of different types of *o*-sounds are disregarded: Spenser 1,880 syllables; Milton 1,757 syllables. In my attempts to identify cases of alliteration and assonance I have been guided primarily by the researches of H. C. Wyld and H. Kökeritz on the pronunciation of sixteenth and seventeenth century English.

identity. Its effect is greater, however, since it need not compete
with any end rhymes. The fairy-fury, foul-full, fierce-force type
of uniformly framed vowels is mostly used to link different
lines but with a controlled power of sound and of semantic suggestion that goes beyond Spenser:

> Of Mans *First* Diso*bedien*ce, and the Fruit
> Of that *Forbidden* Tree. . . .

> And to the *fierce* contention brought along
> Innumerable *force* of Spirits arm'd. . . .

These are nearly all negative features which in themselves could
hardly ensure any great poetic effectiveness. What they do, however, is to make even a slight relaxation of such restrictions immediately felt. Repetitions acquire a rarity value. Echoes become
audible over a distance of several lines even when there is no
correspondence in their metrical positions. Accumulated echoes
attain a force of reverberation seldom achieved in *The Faerie
Queene.* A comparison of two passages closely similar in some
of their wording and imagery may help to realize the difference.
Spenser is nearly at his most vigorous in describing the rage
of the Dragon wounded by the Redcrosse Knight:

> For griefe thereof, and divelish despight,
> From his infernall fournace forth he threw
> Huge flames, that dimmed all the heavens light,
> Enrold in duskish smoke and brimstone blew . . . (I,xi,44)

Milton's Satan looks at hell for the first time after his fall into
the abyss:

> At once as far as Angels kenn he views
> The dismal Situation waste and wilde:
> A dungeon horrible, on all sides round
> As one great Furnace flam'd, yet from those flames
> No light, but rather darkness visible
> Serv'd only to discover sights of woe . . . (I,59–64)

It would be difficult to decide which series of alliterations is more forcible in itself—Spenser's "*F*rom his in*f*ernall *f*ournace *f*orth he threw Huge *f*lames" or Milton's "As one great *F*urnace *f*lam'd, yet *f*rom those *f*lames." They are deceptively alike. Yet there is at least one cardinal difference. This is the first case in *Paradise Lost* of alliterative accumulation on such a scale with sounds of such intensity, whereas Spenser has already been prodigal in filling his lines with repeated consonants to suggest the fierceness of the struggle with the Dragon: "High *b*randishing his *b*right dew-*b*urning *b*lade," "The *d*eadly *d*int his *d*ulled senses all *d*ismaid," "With *f*owle en*f*ou*l*dred smoke and *f*lashing *f*ire," and so forth. So, there is in Spenser hardly any heightening of intensity. He barely succeeds in maintaining a level already reached, which tends to be slightly lowered with every new use of the same stylistic moves. In the Miltonic passage, on the other hand, even such relatively distant correspondences as "A *D*ungeon horri*b*le" and "*d*arkness visi*b*le" contribute to the total impression of definite but finely graded design. What Milton has added, much as painters do by shading, is the dimension of depth. Indeed, his treatment of sound exactly corresponds to the scene he describes. In the deep gloom of hell nothing is clearly distinguishable except the flames, the source of light, however ghostlike. It is on the flames of hell that Milton concentrates the greatest phonetic energy. Both visually and aurally they are placed in the center of the picture.

I have paid only occasional attention so far to Spenser's and Milton's manner of arranging their line endings. Contrasts similar to those already observed, only frequently even more pronounced, will appear as we look more closely at this aspect of their treatment of sound.

Spenser's original contributions to rhyme arrangement, while not very numerous, are significant. They show above all a desire for firm, conspicuous design and balance, combined with at least some measure of climactic organization. The *Epithalamion* and *Prothalamion* stanzas, despite some variation, always fall into three relatively simply but differently constructed sections leading up to two final couplets, the conclusion of which is emphasized by lengthening the last line. In certain instances, notably at the beginning of the *Epithalamion,* rhyme links connect some of the separate sections. This linking technique is fully exploited in the Spenserian sonnet, apparently imitated from the Scots sonneteers but characteristic of Spenser's leanings. Here it results in uninterrupted continuity through three quatrains, up to the final couplet, which forms the point of culmination. The total impression is one of sinuosity, unbreakable unity, and transparency of construction. These features are intensified in *The Faerie Queene* stanza, the structure of which is exactly like that of the first nine lines of Spenser's sonnets, except for the greater length of the last line. The final couplet here is no longer isolated but is firmly built into the total design, which culminates emphatically in the final Alexandrine.

Milton's inventions in the field of rhyme arrangement are less obvious and transparent, but no less logically conceived. At their best they are much more subtle. He begins with comparatively simple structures, many of which characteristically use the Spenserian device of a climactic Alexandrine. Then, save for his sonnets, he almost entirely abandons set stanza forms, using more complex combinations, most of which show a sharply emphasized element of mounting gradation. The growing intricacy of these patterns, however, is always subjected to a firm control over their total structure, while the poet at the same time deftly and most economically contrives to conceal a basic regularity by using what I have called "structural blurs" at decisive points so as to produce an impression of effortless spontaneity. This method, the rudiments of which Milton may have learned from the Italian lyrists, is demonstrated most brilliantly in *Lycidas*. The essential contrasts with Spenser are in Milton's far greater complexity; in his endeavor generally to obscure rather than emphasize an underlying regularity without sacrificing it, while bringing it out with extreme clarity at certain crucial points; in the much wider range of his designs—193 lines of constant variety combined with perfect unity in *Lycidas*—and in a greater capacity for gradual but powerful intensification working towards one all-important peak. Milton seems to be following the very principles that Poe two centuries later appeared to regard as his own personal innovation.

In *Paradise Lost* Milton does much the same in his blank verse that he had done in the rhymed verse of *Lycidas*. Having rejected formal rhyme, he by no means avoids subdued rhymelike effects. Quite on the contrary, he uses them systematically and organizes them carefully, pointing up the mood and matter of his poem both by the phonetic character and by the arrangement of his linked endings. Most of his line-end echoes amount to nothing more than assonance or consonance, but where the effect needs to be intensified, assonance and consonance are combined and may become rhyme. Even the varying frames of mind of the characters are reflected in his methods of patterning. Where mere emotion speaks, the echoes seem disorganized and tend to be heavily massed. Where cool deliberation has the upper hand, they fall into more regular designs, often verging on complete symmetry and extending through long paragraphs. Even so, absolute symmetry seems to be studiously avoided. Something is usually done slightly to upset the balance and thus to prevent an impression of mechanical arrangement. One pattern flows into another, connecting paragraph with paragraph and integrating them all into the infinitely complex larger patterns of the complete books. The variety, expressiveness and delicacy of shading in these patterns, which may include internal echoes and which are generally organized around some dominant central motif, exceed anything done along similar lines by Milton's predecessors in this technique, that is, most of the better writers of blank verse from Surrey onwards.

Spenser's use of a fixed stanza pattern obviously in itself makes such results difficult to achieve. True, phonetic motifs carried from stanza to stanza, as already hinted, provide a larger continuity and more comprehensive patterning for many parts of his poem.[7] Nevertheless, Spenser on the whole seems to do his

[7] Linkages between different stanzas in Spenser are examined in considerable detail in the University of Florida dissertation by Paul Royce Smith, *Studies in Spenser's Rimes* (Gainesville, Florida, 1955).

best to mark the unity and distinctiveness of the individual stanza —for example, by strengthening his rhyme system by means of phonetic links placed more deeply in the line. Internal echoes tend to fall into the same metrical positions. Intense small-scale concentration is brought about in many stanzas by making their first and last rhymes sound alike. Such methods, while often astonishingly delicate in the manner they are applied, in general conspicuously strengthen the part rather than the whole. The microcosm of the stanza is elaborately shaped and consolidated, somewhat at the expense of the macrocosm of the episode or canto. This, by comparison with Milton's powerfully centralizing approach, must be called a method of decentralization —a term which, however, should in no way be taken to suggest lack of order or design.

The differences hitherto observed suggest another generalization. Milton's form, ornate and highly stylized as it often is in the established epic fashion of sustained magnificence, seems to me still essentially functional form, that is, within the limits of epic decorum the style—including the handling of sound— adapts itself to the varying matter. This may seem an oversimplified way of putting it, since the expression does not just reflect the matter but colors it and becomes a part of it. Nevertheless, in Milton the matter predominates to an extent that it does not in Spenser. Spenser's manner at times almost appears to be living a life of its own. Much of the matter is there for the sake of the manner: we often feel it to be essentially an item in a demonstration of style. The events, the scenery, the characters have allegorical meaning (when the author does not happen to forget about it) but a great deal in them seems interchangeable. Think of such triplets as Sansloy, Sansfoy, Sansjoy;

Priamond, Diamond, Triamond; Despetto, Decetto, Defetto; of
the knights Parlante, Jocante, Basciante, Bacchante, Noctante,
and many more. The very names suggest that they have barely
a token individuality, that often they are not even distinguishable types but exist for the sake of a geometrically conceived,
highly abstract pattern—the pattern of a pageant that might go
on almost indefinitely. It is the total arrangement of the pattern,
not any single figure, that counts. In such a formalized world of
the imagination in which there is little that is real in the sense
of having individual reality or much weight of its own, Spenser
may frequently play with form without necessarily giving it
more than a semblance of surface meaning and without sub-
ordinating it too strictly to any central motif so long as the unity
of style is sufficiently maintained.

Milton, too, depicts a world the like of which has never been
seen, but it stands for fundamental, often grim, realities, the importance of which he wishes to convey in every line and syllable
of his poem. His epic has a beginning, a middle, and an end,
and an extremely serious purpose to which every part is sub-
servient. Hence, the form is always intended to convey as much
meaning as it can possibly carry, with careful regard for the
total context of the poem. However lovingly the expression may
seem to be handled, its ultimate objective is never beauty alone:
the element of artistic play scarcely ever becomes self-sufficient.
Spenser is "sage and serious" in his basic intent, and his poem
is obviously full of serious moments—often very long moments
—but Milton, we cannot help feeling, is intensely serious throughout.

Let me try to illustrate this by briefly considering a few passages consisting primarily of proper names—an element of style

capable of many functions and much favored by both poets. Both knew how to choose them for sound, but Spenser often comes close to using them for sound alone. In his catalogue of the Nereides towards the end of the wedding pageant of the Thames and the Medway he does not neglect scholarship: he keeps close to his classical sources, retaining most of the epithets, respecting the etymology of the names, and more or less following their original order. But what clearly interests him most is the opportunities that Mombritius' list affords for building a beautiful piece of *bel canto:*

> White hand Eunica, proud Dynamene,
> Joyous Thalia, goodly Amphitrite,
> Lovely Pasithee, kinde Eulimene,
> Light foote Cymothoe, and sweet Melite,
> Fairest Pherusa, Phao lilly white,
> Wondred Agave, Poris and Nesæa,
> With Erato, that doth in love delite,
> And Panopae, and wise Protomedæa,
> And snowy neckd Doris, and milkewhite Galathæa,
>
> Speedy Hippothoe, and chaste Actea,
> Large Lisianassa, and Pronæa sage,
> Evagore, and light Pontoporea,
> And she that with her least word can asswage
> The surging seas, when they do sorest rage,
> Cymodoce, and stout Autonoe,
> And Neso, and Eione well in age,
> And seeming still to smile, Glauconome,
> And she that hight of many heastes Polynome . . .

This is another one of Spenser's circular patterns: the beginning
and conclusion of the passage as well as its middle parts rhyme
with each other. The symmetry is almost mathematically perfect.
Internal echoes abound. The degree of individualization in the
adjectives—adopted by Spenser even though not invented by
him—is mostly slight. Suggestions of charm and beauty, little
differentiated in kind, are piled up. The arrangement is en-
trancing as verbal music. It has its purpose in the total design
of the pageant as a final luminous patch of color, but this purpose is formal. This, as far as that is possible for anything expressed in words of some meaning, is autonomous form—intricate,
rich, most skilfully shaped, but hardly reaching very far beyond
itself.

Nothing of the sort occurs anywhere in Milton's numerous
lists of names, not even in his earliest verse. The specific associations, the historical, geographical, and cultural context are
scrupulously observed; indeed, they come first, even though the
music hardly ever fails. The longest catalogue, that of the fallen
angels in Book I of *Paradise Lost,* in effect constitutes a well-
ordered compendium of heathen mythology; it has its larger
purposes too, for example, that of definitely labeling all paganism
as belonging to the devil's party. The second longest—that of
the kingdoms of the future which Adam sees from the high hill
in Book XI—systematically combines history with geography.
Even when the subject on the face of it is the enchantment of pure
romance, as in the simile in Book I comparing Satan's forces to
the armies of heroic poetry, the order in time of the different
epic cycles alluded to is carefully maintained: we are given a
condensed piece of literary history. Nor is it likely to be due

to mere chance that this orderly presentation so fully agrees with the orthodox military formation of the infernal battalions which Milton emphatically brings to our notice. These sound effects, never in the least distracting our attention from the logically arranged matter, are so discreet as almost to seem accidental:

> And all who since, Baptiz'd or Infidel
> Jousted in Aspramont or Montalban,
> Damasco, or Marocco, or Trebisond. . . .

Damasco, Marocco, Trebisond, Montalban, Aspramont: parts of these names almost rhyme, but we need to strain our ear a little to notice the fact: this is deliberately muted music. It is muted to avoid any interference with a full realization of the meaning in all its implications.

Spenser is of course a man of the Renaissance, but in Continental terms we should, in defiance of chronology, feel inclined to call him a quattrocentist rather than a cinquecentist. He is still very close to the Middle Ages, no matter how much he may have learned from Tasso or Ariosto. His artistic approach, with his relative disregard of large-scale concentration and subordination, is pre–Neo-Aristotelian. Ariosto, at least in the way he treats his episodes and individual scenes, comes closer to Aristotle's standards: he draws his subjects more distinctly in the round. Spenser's formal skill, especially his handling of symmetry and balance, may owe much to the Italians of the High Renaissance, but he has not yet acquired, or does not care to apply, the art of perspective: we see foreground but little background, as in medieval romances and paintings. The care with which he elaborates the individual stanza or minor pattern

almost defies belief. For parallels we should have to turn to
such a poem as *The Pearl* or, to continue our excursions into
another art, to the illustrations found in medieval illuminated
manuscripts. His joy in the bright and the immediately perceptible leads us into the same chronological context. He loved
Chaucer, but was much less able to resist the attraction of alliterative flashes woven into long series of sparkling designs. In
this respect his art points to a more archaic stage of development
than Chaucer's.

Milton, it goes without saying, as an artist had absorbed very
nearly all that the Renaissance could teach him, and his art points
beyond it. He understood Aristotle better than many of his
most erudite contemporaries did, and knew the value of concentration and firm unity as well as of a style from which one
could both descend and ascend, always keeping something in
reserve. His avoidance of strict symmetry, of very obvious patterning, is post-High Renaissance. Here Tasso may in some
measure have shown him the way, but Milton's gift for displays of mounting strength far exceeds that of Tasso. In this
respect his only rival is Shakespeare, but Milton's method is
more learned and elaborate: he fully utilizes all the lessons in
intricate formal design that he has learned from the more academic poetry of the Renaissance both at home and abroad. His
advantage compared with his models is in his superior genius
for comprehensive organization and in his ability to kindle it
with a new, purposeful energy. In the art of subduing in order
to enhance effectively, the nearest parallel to him is found in the
work of an exact contemporary of his about whom he probably
knew nothing, Rembrandt van Rijn: the latter's concentration

of light on only one point against a background of subtly patterned twilight is, in its manner as well as in its results, the precise pictorial equivalent of Milton's phonetic chiaroscuro with its centers of blazing intensity.

HAROLD WHITEHALL

From Linguistics to Poetry

AS MATHEMATICAL ANALYSIS is basic to the physical sciences, so linguistic analysis is basic to literary criticism. This is particularly true today when criticism, long considered a part of philosophy, is being pursued by the majority of the "New Critics" as an art based on the study of the literary effects of language. Moreover, both criticism and linguistics, in their modern phases, are structuralistic in attitude, both commenced their present trends of development about 1917, and both matured about 1948 to some degree, side by side. Yet because American structural linguistics has been concerned mainly with the description of unwritten languages as expressed in an esoteric and quantized symbolism, our own linguistics and our own criticism have only recently come into intimate contact, first at the joint Linguistic Institute—School of Letters seminars first held at Indiana University in 1952 and continued in following years.

First feelers towards contact between linguistics and criticism—not at all tentative—were put out by the so-called "formalist" and "structuralist" critics of Czechoslovakia, eastern Germany,

and Russia during the late twenties and early thirties. Their
efforts resulted directly in a brilliant series of books on rhyme,
sound-patterns, and metrics and indirectly in an abstruse but
important work, *Das literarische Kunstwerk* (1931), in which
the Polish critic-philosopher, Roman Ingarden, using the phe-
nomenologist techniques of Husserl, banished the form-content
dichotomy, and regarded a work of literary art as consisting
of a series of interlocking levels ("norms") commencing with
the linguistic surface level and ending with the metaphysical.
His notions, somewhat paraphrased, are still useful, and provide
a vertical dimension by which poetry is best approached:

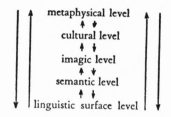

Meanwhile, those linguists concerned with the structure of the
English language, chiefly American, had worked more and more
with a horizontal concept common to behavioristic psychology
and communication theory:

sender ⟶ message ⟶ receiver

Regarding the behavior of *sender* and *receiver* as outside the
scope of their science, they concentrated on the formal characteristics of the message, trying to reduce their consideration of
meaning to differential meaning, that is, to the fact the form
A differs in some semantic respects from form B. Whatever the

virtues of this limitation, which is enforced to some degree by anthropological and psychological inadequacies, it has at least resulted in the creation of a new social science which for rigid definition, development of workable units, and strict methodology is at present the envy of all other social sciences, if sometimes the despair of the Humanities.

Here I propose to combine a modified adaptation of Ingarden's vertical dimension with the American linguist's horizontal dimension, as follows:

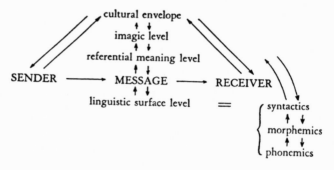

With such a scheme, it is possible to delimit the various possible approaches to the study of poetry: 1) traditional literary scholarship, chiefly, though not always entirely, concerned with the sender and receiver in reaction with the cultural envelope; 2) the "New Criticism," chiefly concerned with the imagic and referential meaning (semantic) levels; 3) a possible "social psychological" criticism—as yet merely nascent—concerned with the estimation of the reactions of the receiver within the social envelope; 4) linguistic criticism, primarily concerned with the lowest, the linguistic surface level, and providing a foundation upon which the traditional literary scholar, the "New Critic," and the social psychology critic must inevitably, sooner or later, erect their theoretical edifices and their analyses. Otherwise their mansions would not have, as previously they have never had, an adequate basement. What all this implies, of course, is that the proper exegesis of poetry demands either the attention of such men of variegated learning as Croce or Erich Auerbach, or—since most of us are far more limited—of a team of experts, working not against each other but with each other, and comprised of a traditional literary scholar, a "New Critic," a social psychologist, and a linguist. That such a team has never been envisaged or assembled is one of the tragedies of contemporary American literary criticism.

One must realize then both the potentialities and the restrictions of what I have called the "linguistic criticism" of poetry. Some things it can do very well indeed—far better, in fact, than ever before: 1) it can elucidate phonemically and sub-phonemically the sound-patterns used structurally and mosaically in poetry; 2) it can phonemically reproduce such sound-patterns as were used in past ages; 3) it can provide an analysis of morphemic and syntactic structure against which "the organized violence done to language" can be projected and compared; 4) within the framework of ascertained syntax, it can provide metrical analyses scientifically correlated with the structure of any language; 5) it can provide the scientific bases for the study of poetical stylistics; 6) now, or in the near future, it may be able to provide a distributional and connotational approach to the analysis of imagery and symbolism. Only the exigencies and uncertainties of time events prevent me from claiming that sooner or later the methods now used in isolating phonemes and morphemes will eventually allow us to quantize "referential meaning" with the same structural simplicities and to the same effect. When that time comes, what is now called "semantics" may become if not linguistic, at least truly metalinguistic. Within the limits of this paper, not all of these potentialities of linguistic criticism can be fully explored. All I can hope to do is to give a brief sampling of a few.

Sound-Pattern. Here we may take as the basic linguistic frame the formula c-v-c in which "c" means any consonant or consonant cluster and "v" any vowel or diphthong, i.e., any recurrent vowel and semivowel sequence. Repetitions of any elements in this formula may be either structural or mosaic (i.e., decorative) according to the nature of the language and its tradition of poetry. Word-repetition, found in Old English, Welsh, Irish, and many other poetic traditions repeats the same unvaried word as a primary structural factor with the same denotational semantic spectrum but with connotational spectra forced on it by its contextual environment. Usually the word occurs three times within relatively few lines: in the Old English "Dream of the Cross," and in the Dylan Thomas "In my craft or sullen art:" however, the incept and coda reiterate their word-repetitions to produce an orbicular structure. *Rich-rhyme,* common in French and other easily rhymed languages, fairly common in Chaucer, frowned on in Modern English, repeats the same phonemic formula but with different semantic spectra, as in English *mete, meet, meat. Alliteration,* the principal factor of poetic structure in early Germanic and some Middle English poetry, repeats either the first c or the v at predetermined intervals. Here it is structural.

In later English poetry it is, on the whole, mosaic except in some of Hopkins's poems, in Dylan Thomas, and (possibly) in Swinburne. *Inverse-Rhyme,* apparently rather rare in the world's literary cultures, repeats the first c-v. *Consonance,* increasingly common as a mosaic device in modern English poetry, repeats the formula c-c. *Assonance,* frequently used as a structural device by such Welsh-inspired poets as Dylan Thomas, Wilfred Owen, and Gerard Manley Hopkins, and found also in early Spanish and Catalan poetry, repeats -v- sometimes at the ends of the lines, sometimes internally according to predetermined patterns.

Rhyme repeats the formula -v-c- often at line endings, but in a good many poetic traditions, internally with cross-reference to the line endings. Rhyme is in a sense the most mysterious of all the sound patterns. It is non-indigenous to most European literatures and has apparently been acquired by us from some South Mid-Asian Semitic language by the process of acculturation. It is found in Chinese poetry, but is apparently absent from the American Indian languages of this continent, with one notable exception in which, of course, it may have been adapted from English. The occurrence of internal rhyme in many literary traditions may be either structural or mosaic. Certainly in the Celtic traditions the rigid pattern of occurrence would indicate that it is structural. In English, rhyme seems to have had three periods of development. It is mosaic in Old English poetry with the exception of the so-called "Rhyming Poem." In the Middle English period, it is alternated with alliteration particularly by those poets influenced by the French tradition, aided and abetted by the introduction of French words into the language with stress on the last syllable. In early Modern English, rhyme was relatively easy because of the operations of the Great Sound Shift, though even here Shakespeare is quite capable of rhyming one vowel with another if the following consonant belongs to the same phonemic class. Because of the developments of the English sound system from roughly 1750 onwards, rhyme has become increasingly difficult in Modern English and, for structural purposes, has been increasingly deserted in favor of "eye" rhymes, slant rhymes, consonance and assonance. When a structural device hinders rather than helps the poet, that is to be expected.

As to the elucidation of poetic phonology during the periods ranging roughly from 1550 to 1750, linguistic criticism can give a very simple and necessary explanation. We are fortunate that Modern English spelling spells roughly the very late Middle English of the Caxton era and that from 1588 onwards we have relatively accurate phonetic renditions of what phonemic structure of the language actually was. Phonetic complexities aside, any critic can reconstruct the pronunciation of this particular period of poetry with a minimum of trouble if he follows the underlying diagram.

The East Midland Middle English vowel system seems to have consisted of five simple vowels and twelve complex nuclei arranged in the phonetic pattern shown by the following keywords:

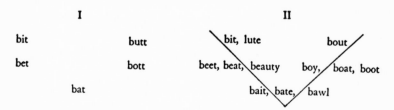

I					II			
bit		butt		bit, lute			bout	
bet		bott		beet, beat,	beauty	boy,	boat, boot	
	bat			bait,	bate,	bawl		

Or, to give phonemic renderings:

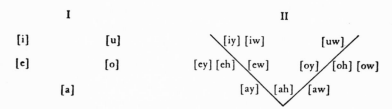

The first phase of the Great Sound Shift, which must have been very early, affected only the complex nuclei outside the triangle and left the pillars of the system intact. It consisted of a systematic interchange of glides whereby [h] became [y] or [w], and [y] or [w] became [h], in each case with a tensing and raising of the vowel. Thus: [ey] in *beet* became [ih]; [eh] in *beat* became [ey]; [ay] in *bait* became [eh]; [aw] in *bawl* became [oh]; [oh] in *boat* became [ow]; and [ow] in *boot* became [uh].

The second phase of the Great Sound shift involved all the simple vowels and all the complex nuclei left unchanged by the preceding phase. It did not, at first, occasion any change in the glides of the complex nuclei and must be considered essentially a vowel change. It may be described as a tendency of all vowels to swerve around in a clockwise centripetal arc *whenever favorable environments encourage this.*

To this we owe the developments of the new vowels 'schwa,' [ï], the shift of [o] to [a], and of [a] to [æ] before consonants in close contact, the initial development of [iy] in *bite* to [ïy],

and of [uw] in *bout* to ['schwa' plus w], the coalescence of the
sound classes represented by *meat* and *meet,* and a dozen other
features of Early Modern English and the Modern English
dialects.

What has been said above by no means exhausts the possibilities
of a linguistic analysis of sound pattern. A phoneme is basically
a chord of acoustic features which with neighboring phonemes
may repeat certain features, as a musical chord repeats certain
notes. In such a passage as Tennyson's famous "The moan of
doves in immemorial elms/ And murmuring of innumerable
bees . . ." the unusual number of resonant consonants is quite
obvious. What the linguist would point out is the preponderance
of the "schwa" vowel, and the preponderance of the acoustic
features of continuousness and voicing. These have a good deal
to do with the particular effect of the pattern on the reader.

Metrics. Metrics depends upon multiple factors: 1) sub-glottal
and supra-glottal organic activity; 2) the syntactical framework
within which it operates; 3) borrowing from other languages;
4) the theories which have been elaborated to explain it. In
English, it is conditioned partly by the structure of the language
and partly by the tradition inherited in the seventeenth century
from France.

English appears to have four kinds of loudness (stress) closely
associated with what should be called disjuncture but is usually
called juncture; that is, interruption of the normal transition between phonemes. We may characterize the stress as maximum
($\diagup$), major ($\wedge$), minor ($\diagdown$), and minimal ($\smile$) for metrical
purposes. A syllable may then be defined as the domain of any
stress level. The traditional "ideal" metrical patterns of much
English verse—patterns based on the two-level contrast of stressed

versus unstressed syllables—have been "orchestrated" since Marlowe by a poetic adaptation of the actual four-level contrast of speech. In this adaptation, the primary stress ($/$) always indicates a metrically stressed syllable and the weak stress ($\smile$) a metrically unstressed syllable; the two medial stresses ($\wedge$) and ($\setminus$), however, indicate metrically stressed syllables if surrounded by weaker stresses and metrically unstressed syllables if surrounded by stronger stresses. Hence: The lowing herd/winds slowly/ o'er the lea.

Needless to say, this analysis is not complete either for English or for very many languages. The linguist, on the basis of his experiences, is able to suggest a typical outline usable in comparative prosodics. In this, the first distinction would be drawn between syllabic and non-syllabic rhythms. The simplest type of the former is the non-configurational verse of early Vedic and of some Hungarian folk poems—rhymed or assonanced lines with no other prosodic feature than a fixed number of syllables. In the sense that certain syllables are made prominent by weighting them with a configurational feature, all other syllabic rhythms are configurational. Classical Chinese isotonic verse weights with high pitches, alternately fixed and moving, ,n every second syllable; quantitative verse weights with length, basically on the principle (at least in Greek and Sanskrit) that closed syllables are long, open syllables short; isoaccentual, or, as it is often called, isosyllabic rhythm weights with stress. Of the non-syllabic rhythms, the first, found typically in Old Testament Hebrew verse and in some, though not all, "free verse" is isosyntactic—the recurrent factor is repetition of the same syntactic construction, usually a phrase or clause, in strictly parallel sequences. The other type is the isochronic, in which the rhythm depends on equal time-lapses between primary stresses. This, probably the most varied rhythm that prosody has yet discovered, completes the inventory of prosodic types.

Prosody is, in fact, a rather complex subject. True, pure configurational, isotonic, quantitative, isoaccentual, isosyntactic, and —most commonly—isochronic rhythms do occur, but frequent cross-cultural borrowings of prosodic types have very often resulted, as in English, in the development of rhythms of great contrapuntal complexity.

Syntax and Stylistics. English syntax can be resolved into recurrent partials of six word-groups. These are very important in poetry, since the poet very often introduces new types of word-groups and uses the normal word-groups ambiguously for their shock value. A good poet expects the reader to participate with his ultimate imagination in reaction to what has been written down. We require norms, therefore, against which the divagations of the poet can be estimated. The following scheme shows the principal word-groups of normal expository English prose; against it may be projected those violences of syntax which we expect and indeed hope to find in poetry.

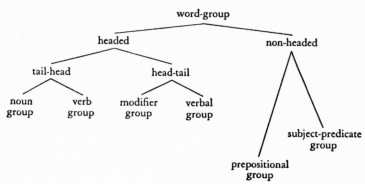

Since metrics always operates within syntactical frameworks, pointing up the syntactical units, consideration of both the normal syntactic structure of English and the variations from them is essential to the linguistic analysis of poetry. All poets have favorite word-groups which they manipulate as the grounds of their metrical schemes. Moreover, the style of any given period of English poetry is mainly to be resolved on the repeated structural occurrence of some of these groups, or, quite frequently, of the ambiguous use of them. Since certain word-groups constitute English sentences, they exhaust the linguist's direct contribution to the study of English poetry. The strict linguist goes no further than consideration of the sentence.

Over and above all this, I am not quite sure what the linguist can do for the appreciation of poetry. It is only a question of time before he moves into a scientific study of symbolism. He already knows most of the facts, if not exactly the best expression, of the alphabet of kinesics (gestures), and of voice-qualifiers. If, as I suspect, the ultimate proof of pudding is the eating, if poetry ever returns, as I think it will return, to virtuosic rendering by a virtuoso, then the horse of poetry will be led into the stables of Parnassus not by a "New Critic," and not at all by a traditional literary scholar, but by a linguist. Who fodders it afterwards is not my or our present concern.

Supervising Committee, the English Institute, 1956

LEWIS LEARY (1956), *Chairman, Columbia University*

ABBIE FINDLAY POTTS (1956), *Rockford College*

RENE WELLEK (1956), *Yale University*

HARRY LEVIN (1957), *Harvard University*

HELEN NEILL MCMASTER (1957), *Sarah Lawrence College*

JAMES E. THORPE (1957), *Princeton University*

G. ARMOUR CRAIG (1958), *Amherst College*

RICHARD L. GREENE (1958), *Wesleyan University*

MURIEL HUGHES (1958), *University of Vermont*

EUGENE M. WAITH, *Secretary, Yale University*

The Program

CONFERENCES

I. THE EDITOR AND HIS AUDIENCE
Directed by ALLEN T. HAZEN, *Columbia University*

1. The American Pelican Shakespeare: Editing for Students and the General Public
   ALFRED HARBAGE, *Harvard University*

2. Editing the Letters of Letter-Writers
   ROBERT HALSBAND, *Hunter College*

3. The *Life of Johnson* and Boswell's Manuscript
   MARSHALL WAINGROW, *Yale University*

4. Problems of Interpretation for an Editor of *Ulysses*
   EDMUND L. EPSTEIN, *Columbia University*

II. THE SHORT NOVEL
Directed by DOROTHY VAN GHENT, *University of Vermont*

1. Creative Principles in the Novel
   SUSANNE LANGER, *Connecticut College*

2. Character and Action in the Short Novel: James, Conrad, and Some Contemporaries
   R. W. B. LEWIS, *Rutgers University*

3. Form as Discriminator in Lawrence's Short Novels
   MONROE ENGEL, *Harvard University*

4. Problems of the Short Novel from the Point of View of the Writer
   HOWARD NEMEROV, *Bennington College*

III. PERIPHERIES OF LITERATURE

Directed by PHILIP WHEELWRIGHT, *University of California, Riverside*

1. Biography and Literature
   EDWIN FUSSELL, *Claremont Graduate School*

2. Psychology and Literature
   FREDERICK J. HOFFMAN, *University of Wisconsin*

3. Religion and Literature
   NATHAN A. SCOTT, JR., *University of Chicago*

4. Philosophy and Literature
   PHILIP WHEELWRIGHT, *University of California, Riverside*

IV. MUSIC AND POETRY

Directed by FREDERICK W. STERNFELD, *Dartmouth College*

1. Lexis and Melos
   NORTHROP FRYE, *Victoria College, Toronto*

2. Words into Music: The Composer's Approach to the Text
   EDWARD T. CONE, *Princeton University*

3. Poetry and Music: Joyce's *Ulysses*
   FREDERICK W. STERNFELD, *Dartmouth College*

4. *Musica Mundana* and *Twelfth Night*
   JOHN HOLLANDER, *Harvard University*

EVENING MEETING SEPTEMBER 6

The Scholar Critic

JACQUES BARZUN, Dean of the Graduate Faculties, *Columbia University*

Recital of Secular Music of the Twelfth through the Seventeenth Centuries

DAVID FULLER, *Harpsichord*

ANNE HOLLANDER, *Mezzo-Soprano*

JOHN HOLLANDER, *Lute*

ROBERT SIMON, *Baritone*

Registrants, 1956

Ruth M. ADAMS, University of Rochester; Leonard ALBERT, Hunter College; Gellert S. ALLEMAN, Rutgers University at Newark; Marcia E. ALLENTUCK, Columbia University; G. L. ANDERSON, New York University; Liberty Marian ANTALIS, Steubenville College; Mother Thomas AQUINAS, College of New Rochelle; James Richard BAIRD, Connecticut College; Sheridan BAKER, University of Michigan; C. Lombardi BARBER, Amherst College; Phyllis BARTLETT, Queens College; Jacques BARZUN, Columbia University; Paul L. BENNETT, Denison University; Carroll G. BOWEN, Oxford University Press; Brother C. Francis BOWERS, Catholic University; Fredson BOWERS, University of Virginia; Reverend John Dominic BOYD, Bellarmine College; Mary Campbell BRILL, West Virginia Wesleyan College; Cleanth BROOKS, Yale University; George Edward BROOKS, Springfield College; Richard A. E. BROOKS, Vassar College; Wentworth K. BROWN, Rensselaer Polytechnic Institute; Margaret M. BRYANT, Brooklyn College; Mrs. W. BRYHER; Brother Fidelian BURKE, Catholic University; Arthur BURKHARD; Sister M. Vincentia BURNS, Albertus Magnus College; Katherine BURTON, Wheaton College; Kathleen Mary BYRNE.

Herbert Thomas Fuller CAHOON, Pierpont Morgan Library; Grace CALDER, Hunter College; Oscar James CAMPBELL, Columbia University; Albert Howard CARTER, University of Arkansas; Hugh C. G.

CHASE; George Peirce CLARK, Northern Illinois State College; Harold Edward CLARK, Saint Lawrence University; James L. CLIFFORD, Columbia University; Robert A. COLBY, Queens College; William Bradley COLEY, Wesleyan University; Ralph Waterbury CONDEE, Pennsylvania State University; Edward T. CONE, Princeton University; Jeannette Alice CONFER, Lycoming College; Frederick W. CONNER, University of Florida; Francis CONNOLLY, Fordham University; Joan Elizabeth CORBETT, University of Richmond; David K. CORNELIUS, Randolph-Macon Woman's College; Roberta D. CORNELIUS, Randolph-Macon Woman's College; Paul CORTISSOZ, Manhattan College; George Armour CRAIG, Amherst College; Lucille CRIGHTON, Gulf Park College; John CROW, King's College, London University; Reverend John V. CURRY, Le Moyne College; Kenneth CURRY, University of Tennessee; Curtis DAHL, Wheaton College; Richard Beale DAVIS, University of Tennessee; Francis X. DEGNEN, Saint John's University; Robert M. DELL, Pace College; Rutherford E. DELMAGE, Saint Lawrence University; Sister Rose Bernard DONNA, College of Saint Rose; Mabel Collins DONNELLY; R. Joel DORIUS, Yale University; Elizabeth DREW, Smith College; E. Catherine DUNN, Catholic University.

Leon EDEL, Washington Square College, New York University; Ursula Elizabeth EDER, Vassar College; Monroe ENGEL, Harvard University; Edmund L. EPSTEIN, Buffalo University; David V. ERDMAN, New York Public Library; Leslie Aaron FIEDLER, Montana State University; Peter Francis FISHER, Royal Military College of Canada; Frank Cudworth FLINT, Dartmouth College; Claude R. FLORY, Florida State University; Stephen F. FOGLE, University of Florida; Robert H. FOSSUM, Beloit College; Elizabeth S. FOSTER, Oberlin College; Frances A. FOSTER, Vassar College; Louis FRAIBERG, Wayne University; Lewis FREED, Purdue University; Albert B. FRIEDMAN, Harvard University; Northrop FRYE, Victoria College, University of Toronto; Edwin Sill FUSSELL, Claremont Graduate School; Paul FUSSELL, Jr., Rutgers University; John Waldhorn GASSNER, Yale University; Katherine Haynes GATCH, Hunter College; Helmut E. GERBER, Lafayette College; Thomas Hungerford GIDDINGS, United States Merchant Marine

Academy; Ray GINGER, Alfred A. Knopf; Douglas GRANT, University of Toronto; James GRAY, Bishop's University; Richard L. GREENE, Wesleyan University; Mary Elizabeth GRENANDER, New York State College for Teachers.

Gordon S. HAIGHT, Yale University; Robert HALSBAND, Hunter College; Victor Michael HAMM, Marquette University; John Anders HANSEN, Jr., University of Tennessee; Alfred B. HARBAGE, Harvard University; Brice HARRIS, Pennsylvania State University; Robin S. HARRIS, University College, University of Toronto; John Augustine HART, Carnegie Institute of Technology; Allen T. HAZEN, Columbia University; Miriam Margaret HEFFERNAN, Brooklyn College; Frederick Whiley HILLES, Yale University; John HINZ, City College of New York; C. Fenno HOFFMAN, Jr., Middlebury College; Frederick J. HOFFMAN, University of Wisconsin; Norman Norwood HOLLAND, Massachusetts Institute of Technology; Anne HOLLANDER; John HOLLANDER, Harvard University; Helene HOOKER, Queens College; Vivian C. HOPKINS, New York State College for Teachers; Donald R. HOWARD, Ohio State University; Muriel J. HUGHES, University of Vermont; Dalma M. HUNYADI, Lewis College; Lawrence W. HYMAN, Brooklyn College; Julia Helen HYSHAM, Skidmore College; Anne C. JOHNSON, Columbia University; Samuel F. JOHNSON, Columbia University; Norman KELVIN, University College, Rutgers University; Charlotte R. KESLER, College of William and Mary; Karl KIRALIS, Saint Lawrence University; John P. KIRBY, Randolph-Macon Woman's College; Rudolf KIRK, Rutgers University; Leo KIRSCHBAUM, Wayne State University; Carl Frederick KLINCK, University of Western Ontario; Murray KRIEGER, University of Minnesota; Frank A. KRUTZKE, Colorado College.

Reverend John P. LAHEY, Fordham University; Victor LANGE, Cornell University; Susanne LANGER, Connecticut College; Reverend Henry St. Clair LAVIN, Fordham University; Natalie Grimes LAWRENCE, University of Miami; Lewis LEARY, Columbia University; Harry LEVIN, Harvard University; Nancy E. LEWIS, Denison University; Richard W. B. LEWIS, Rutgers University; Ellen Douglass LEYBURN, Agnes

Scott College; Marion K. MABEY, University of Connecticut; Mary Reid MCBETH, Indiana State Teachers College; James R. MCCONKEY, Cornell University; Sister Mary Immaculate MCELROY; George Joseph MCFADDEN, Temple University; Kenneth MACLEAN, Victoria College, University of Toronto; Helen Neill MCMASTER, Sarah Lawrence College; Mother C. E. MAGUIRE, Newton College of the Sacred Heart; Leonard F. MANHEIM, City College of New York; Sister Julie MARIE, College of Mount Saint Vincent; Sister Elizabeth MARION, College of Mount Saint Vincent; Florence Gertrude MARSH, Western Reserve University; Mary Hatch MARSHALL, Syracuse University; Thomas F. MARSHALL, Kent State University; Harold C. MARTIN, Harvard University; Louis Lohr MARTZ, Yale University; Vivian H. S. MERCIER, City College of New York; Harrison T. MESEROLE, University of Maryland; Dorothy Siegfrieda MILTON, Ferris Institute; Louie M. MINER; Sister Jeanne Pierre MITTNIGHT, College of Saint Rose; Mother Grace MONAHAN, College of New Rochelle; Howard McCoy MUNFORD, Middlebury College.

Alan NELSON, Union College; Howard NEMEROV, Bennington College; George L. NESBITT, Hamilton College; John W. NICHOL, Denison University; Elizabeth NITCHIE, Goucher College; Reverend William Thomas NOON, Canisius College; Sterling P. OLMSTED, Rensselaer Polytechnic Institute; Reverend Joseph E. O'NEILL, Fordham University; Ants ORAS, University of Florida; James M. OSBORN, Yale University; Thomas OSBORN, Yale University; Marvin A. OWINGS, Clemson College; William Doremus PADEN, University of Kansas; Norman Holmes PEARSON, Yale University; Harry William PEDICORD; Marvin Banks PERRY, Jr., Washington and Lee University; Willard B. POPE, University of Vermont; Henry POPKIN, Brandeis University; Abbie Findlay POTTS, Rockford College; Joseph PRESCOTT, Wayne University; Hereward T. PRICE, University of Michigan; Max PUTZEL, Yale University; Reverend Charles Joaquin QUIRK, Loyola University of the South; Harry H. RANSOM, University of Texas; Isabel Elizabeth RATHBORNE, Hunter College; John K. REEVES, Skidmore College;

Catherine Mifflin REIGART, Brooklyn College; Gertrude B. RIVERS, Howard University; (Mrs.) Jonathan T. RORER; William Kent ROSE, Vassar College; Florence ROSENFELD, Hofstra College; Kenneth Sprague ROTHWELL, University of Cincinnati; Blair ROUSE, Mount Union College.

Mother Marie SAINT RITA, Notre Dame College; Bernard Nicholas SCHILLING, University of Rochester; Sister Mary Thecla SCHMIDT, Seton Hill College; Helene SCHNABEL; Flora Rheta SCHREIBER, New School for Social Research; Nathan A. SCOTT, University of Chicago; Merton M. SEALTS, Jr., Lawrence College; John D. SEELYE, Claremont Graduate School; Frank Eugene SEWARD, Catholic University; Oscar A. SILVERMAN, University of Buffalo; Robert SIMON; Sister Mary Francis SLATTERY, College of Mount Saint Vincent; Nathan Comfort STARR, University of Florida; Erwin R. STEINBERG, Carnegie Institute of Technology; Frederick W. STERNFELD, Oxford University; Helen Larson STEVENS, Illinois Institute of Technology; Allan Henry STEVENSON, Hunt Library; Samuel Emlen STOKES, Jr., Harvard University; William C. STOKOE, Jr., Gallaudet College; George Winchester STONE, Jr., New York University; Bryce THOMAS, Pace College; Craig Ringwalt THOMPSON, Lawrence College; Doris Stevens THOMPSON, Russell Sage College; William Burton TODD, Harvard University; A. Robert TOWERS, Queens College.

Samson O. A. ULLMANN, University of Minnesota; Dorothy Waterman UPTON, Skidmore College; Thomas Hume VANCE, Dartmouth College; Dorothy VAN GHENT, University of Vermont; Ruth G. VAN HORN, Western Michigan College; Hyatt H. WAGGONER, Brown University; Richard Long WAIDELICH, Goucher College; Eugene M. WAITH, Yale University; Charles Child WALCOTT, Queens College; John WALDRON, Georgetown University; Andrew J. WALKER, Georgia Institute of Technology; Reverend Norman WEYAND, Loyola University; Philip E. WHEELWRIGHT, University of California; Mother Elizabeth S. WHITE, Newton College of the Sacred Heart; J. Edwin WHITESELL, University of South Carolina; K. Jerome WILKINSON, Knox College; Edwin Eliott

WILLOUGHBY, Folger Shakespeare Library; William Kurtz WIMSATT, Jr., Yale University; Eleanor M. WITHINGTON, Queens College; Marion WITT, Hunter College; Bertram Lawrence WOODRUFF, West Virginia State College; Samuel K. WORKMAN, Illinois Institute of Technology; Mabel P. WORTHINGTON, Temple University.

Randall Library – UNCW
PE1010 .E5 1956   NXWW
Frye / Sound and poetry.

3049001994422